PAUL SIMON

LET'S PUT AMERICA BACK TO WORK

Bonus Books, Chicago

91   90   89   88   87   5   4   3   2   1

Library of Congress Catalog Card Number: 86-70704

International Standard Book Number: 0-933893-18-3

Bonus Books, Inc.
160 East Illinois Street
Chicago, Illinois 60611

Printed in the United States of America

Dedicated to the unemployed,
who feel unwanted and unnoticed.

CONTENTS

PREFACE

I N HIS FIRST inaugural address, President Ronald Reagan said, "Government is not the solution to our problem, government is the problem."

Government is neither, automatically. Government is a tool that can be used for good purposes or for bad purposes. A hammer can be used for building a house, or it can be used to hit someone in the head. The tool can be used properly or improperly.

This book is an attempt to spell out how government can be used properly to help solve a problem that is sapping the economy and the spirit of the nation.

Unemployment will not disappear by wishing it away, by a policy of drift and hope, by making pious speeches about it. Doing a politically safe ballet dance around the issue will not solve it. We need to march on the problem. This book proposes how we can effectively march on it.

You will find I make frequent references to Illinois. That happens to be my primary base of experience. But what I have learned in Illinois, I am sure I could experience in Maryland or Texas or South Dakota. The examples and the applications are everywhere.

A number of people have helped me produce this book, though the responsibility for the views expressed and any errors are mine. Playing a key role through the development of the manuscript was my secretary, Jackie Williams, whose skills are surpassed only by her patience. Others who have helped include my wife Jeanne Hurley Simon, my daughter Sheila Simon, my son Martin Simon, my brother Arthur Simon, and the following: Rafael Anglada, David Axelrod, Judith Bendewald, Alan S. Blinder, Heather Booth, David Bucher, David Carle, Floyd Fithian, John H. Gibbons, Katherine Gillman, Ron Haskins, Pam Huey, Milton Katz, Ellen Meyer, Hyman Minsky, Richard Moe, Patricia O'Brien, Ray Quintanilla, Bernard Rapoport, Marcus Raskin, Kathryn Saltmarsh, Bettylu Saltzman, Roger Semerad, Lester Thurow, and Judy Wagner.

If the book sells well, but there is no resultant action, the book will be a failure. If, however, only a few copies sell, but those who read it are compelled to act, I will consider the writing of it a great success.

—*Paul Simon*

SECTION ONE

THE ALMOST
UNSEEN
GROWING
THREAT

Chapter One

The Problem

THE UNITED STATES of America works, but it must be made to work better.

A massive waste of humanity is taking place each day, and that waste is slowly but certainly eroding our economic future.

The nation heard editorial cheers when the unemployment rate dropped to 7.2 percent for 1985, but between the Great Depression and 1980 there were only two years (1975 and 1976) when the unemployment rate was that high. Although there has been some month-to-month variation in joblessness, the overall unemployment rate has increased by more than one percentage point each decade since 1950. My colleague Senator Daniel P. Moynihan has accurately noted, "Rates of unemployment that were thought intolerable in the early 1960s are thought unattainable in the 1980s."[1]

Under the leadership of President Harry Truman, Congress passed the Full Employment Act of 1946, making a commitment in words to provide employment opportunities to all Americans. Truman then was worried about one million people unemployed. Forty years later, with ten million people unemployed, the hope and the promise of that act remain unfulfilled.

Is rising unemployment part of our destiny?

Part of the answer to that question rests with the ability or inability of our economy to expand, to compete in an increasingly competitive world.

President Ronald Reagan appointed the chief executive officer of one of this nation's major corporations, John A. Young of Hewlett-Packard, to head a task force to study America's industrial competitiveness and future compared to other countries. When the report came back with a gloomy assessment, the President chose to downplay it. Instead of accepting it personally, he let Secretary of Commerce Malcolm Baldridge quietly receive the report. The administration obviously hoped the message would slip into oblivion without notice.

That task force told us bluntly: "Our ability to compete in world markets is eroding. Growth in U. S. productivity lags far behind that of our foreign competitors. Real hourly compensation of our work force is no longer improving. U. S. leadership in world trade is declining."[2]

That assessment is one small part of mounting evidence of economic problems for the future—and mounting unemployment—if we simply continue to drift instead of actively, aggressively constructing a better tomorrow.

Two Harvard professors did a study and concluded: "For some fifteen years the United States has been losing its capacity to compete in the world economy. . . . Unless the United States reexamines and modifies its basic economic strategy, it will no longer be able simultaneously to lead the Western Alliance, increase the domestic standard of living, and maintain existing transfer payments to improve the distribution of income."[3] A respected industrial leader warns, "We are dismantling our industrial capability and constructing in its place a supermarket for imports."[4]

Economist Lester Thurow states, "America's fundamental problems remain unresolved. The long-run trend rate of growth of productivity is still low. America is every day becoming less competitive in world markets. Current policies are not capable of running the U. S. economy at full employment without inflation for any lengthy period of time."[5] He adds: "If present trends continue, America's standard of living will fall relative to those of the world's new industrial leaders, and it will become simply another country—Egypt, Greece, Rome, Portugal, Spain, England—that once led the world economically but no longer does."[6]

Some respected observers have virtually given up. They believe the United States has economic hardening of the arteries, and that our situation will inevitably get worse and worse. A biographer of theologian Reinhold Niebuhr writes of Niebuhr's last years: "Honors bestowed in recognition of past powers and achievements must have made his present quandary all the more painful to contemplate."[7] The wrinkled forehead crowd believes that this is a description of our nation, that our past is glorious, but that our present problems are but a foretaste of the pain to come. Yes, it is true, they admit, that average male income has moved from $2,961 in 1950 to $17,236 in 1984, that average female income has moved from $1,296 in 1950 to $12,567 in 1984, and that average income for the various minorities has improved significantly over those years. But, they add, the growth in unemployment and the recent marked slowing of income growth were inevitable. We have reached our zenith, they assert, though they may say it obliquely, not wanting to offend the rest of us.

Such a pessimistic analysis is flawed, if we make it flawed, because it fails to acknowledge the tremendous potential in the human resources of this nation. We need to channel those resources more effectively, more creatively. We need to take corrective action. A future with little or no growth is no more inevitable for our country than is starvation inevitable for someone holding ten $100 bills, living next to a supermarket, but not recognizing the value of the money. That person must recognize the value of his or her resources and use them effectively.

We have to recognize our resources and use them effectively.

Nothing restricts the future as much as our failure to use our human resources more fully. Why has Japan made such tremendous strides, moving from income that was 5 percent of the average American's income in 1950, to 67 percent in 1984? Japan, a nation the size of California and half our population, has few natural resources. Yet Japan has surpassed most nations in economic growth through developing ideas and human potential. Japan has announced a goal of having the world's highest per capita income by the year 2000, and few contest that possibility.

For the United States to fail to understand the need to develop ideas and human resources much more fully is not simply economic folly, not simply lacerating ourselves with self-inflicted wounds, it is causing untold and needless agony across this good and rich land. Unfortunately, most of us don't see the agony. In the play named for the lead character, Zorba draws laughs when he says the obvious to a man he meets, "We are strangers because we do not know each other." The agony of joblessness is a stranger to most Americans because we do not know it personally. We may experience it slightly through seasonal unemployment, through a temporary layoff, through a temporary transition period of a week or two from one job to another, but not the hard, real thing. Even if we do not encounter joblessness in its full harshness, it touches us every day in a multitude of ways. We face the indirect spinoffs from unemployment: high crime rates, and tax money going for welfare and prisons and unemployment compensation. But, for most of us, the confrontation with unemployment's grimness is distant, indirect. The ugly realities do not penetrate most middle-class homes.

Unemployment leads to poverty, and the poverty statistics are not pleasant. In 1984 one in every seven Americans lived in families that fell below the poverty line of $10,609 for a family of four.

In 1968 the poorest fifth of U. S. families had 91 percent of the money needed for basic requirements, but fifteen years later that had fallen to 60 percent. Most of the poor are white, but blacks are three times as likely as whites to live in poverty; Hispanics are more than twice as likely. Thirty-four percent of those living in female-headed families are poor. The only good news in the poverty statistics is that the percentage of elderly Americans living in poverty is declining. Older Americans are being lifted by Social Security and programs like Supplemental Security Income. But those over sixty-five are only 14 percent of our population. For the non-elderly poor in our midst the main answer must be jobs.

And we are not just talking about statistics.

Ervin and Jane Donohue came to a rural county courthouse to see me. Snow was lightening the landscape, and the old courthouse was chilly as we talked. Ervin is forty-two, his wife appears to be a few years younger. Their clothes are clean but simple and well-worn; they both talk with the slight twang people associate with the hills of deep southern Illinois.

"Neither of us can find a job," Ervin says, "and we have a fifteen-year-old daughter who is ashamed of the clothes she has to wear to high school; we have a thirteen-year-old daughter who has a serious leg and hip deformity, but we can't afford the devices the doctor says will help her; and we have a ten-year-old boy. I drew unemployment compensation until it ran out, and now I'm on welfare. I figure we draw about seventy-five cents an hour, plus food stamps, and we're trying to live on that."

"How do you heat your home?" I asked.

"We bought a second-hand wood stove, and the wife and me and the kids walk along the highway and pick up wood."

"Could you get to Harrisburg [a town of about 10,000 people thirty miles away] if I could get you a part-time job there?"

"I'd get there somehow. I don't know how, but I'd hitchhike if I had to. Right now the tires on our old car are so bad I don't know if we'll make it home. But I'll do anything to get a job."

That's reality.

When I visited the World Color Press plant at Mt. Vernon, Illinois, a man, perhaps thirty-two years old, was standing at the entrance holding a bicycle and asked, "Could I speak to you for sixty seconds?" I listened as he spelled out his desperate search for a job and then added, "I couldn't afford any gasoline for my car to come here, so I borrowed the neighbor boy's bike and rode in fourteen miles to see you."

That's reality.

I don't know how many women in their fifties I have talked to, stranded by husbands through death or separation or divorce, who suddenly need to make a living for the first time in their lives. No marketable skills. Lonely. Almost helpless.

That's reality.

But the realities run deeper than these personal problems. There are staggering effects on our society in a host of larger ways. The statistics are fairly simple. Roughly 7 percent unemployment, but that does not count two to three million Americans who are working part-time, who would like to be working full-time. If you work one hour a week, you are counted as employed. The 7 percent does not count what the Bureau of Labor Statistics calls "the discouraged worker," the person who has simply given up, who is no longer looking for a job. He or she may be in an area of high unemployment, or fifty-five years old and a longtime worker in a dress factory now shut down or a coal mine that has closed. These people show up for months at the local employment office and at other places to look for jobs, but eventually they just give up—on themselves, on their future and on our society. They are "the discouraged workers," and there are more than a million of them.

In all, we have at least ten million people unemployed or significantly underemployed (working two days or less a week when they want to work full time). Ten million people is almost twice the population of Switzerland. If Switzerland suddenly would have no employment, the U. S. government would galvanize our resources to help the Swiss people. Lions Clubs and Women's Clubs and churches and synagogues would volunteer help. As they should! But when more than twice the employable population of Switzerland is unemployed within our own borders, we have yet to make it a matter of major national concern. It is not a high priority for us. One-third of that ten million number fortunately are unemployed for less than thirty days, but the average length of unemployment had grown to more than fifteen weeks by 1985.

The figure of ten million unemployed is higher than the rosy official estimates of eight million but lower than the estimates of others. Dr. Leon Keyserling, once Chairman of the Council of Economic Advisers for President Truman, believes the accurate figure today is closer to twelve million.[8] No one knows the number precisely. Ten million unemployed may understate joblessness slightly, but it is probably close to accurate.

From 1979 to 1984, 11.5 million Americans lost their jobs because plants had shut down or moved or modernized production techniques or because of decreased demand. Of that 11.5 million, more than a million have simply dropped out of the labor force. They are no longer counted among the unemployed. Of those who were able to find new jobs, over half found themselves earning less money.

The federal government estimates that more than two million women who were homemakers have suddenly found themselves divorced or widowed or abandoned.[9] They generally have little or no paid work experience, in the sense of a nine-to-five job. Almost half of these women either are alone in their poverty or are part of a family with total family income below $10,000. They often have an extremely difficult time getting a job.

Women in general have a tougher time. Listen to a witness before a Senate committee: ''Twenty-three percent of adult females are illiterate as compared with 17 percent of adult males.... Half of the heads of household below the poverty level (who are mostly female) cannot read an eighth grade book, and a third of the mothers receiving AFDC [Aid to Families with Dependent Children] are functionally illiterate.... Among female heads of household with educational attainment below a high school diploma, 75 percent were living in poverty in 1981, as compared with 34 percent of households headed by males with equivalent educational attainment.''[10]

Herbert Stein, Chairman of the Council of Economic Advisers under Presidents Richard Nixon and Gerald Ford, wrote in the *Wall Street Journal* about the ''frightening concentration [of unemployment] on the young and minorities,'' but he bolstered a myth that is unfortunately all too often believed: ''On September 14, 1977, I wrote an article on this page entitled, 'Full Employment at Last.' The rate was then 7 percent. My evidence was direct personal observation that the 'Help Wanted' signs remained un-. answered for months at a time while some employed people acted as if they had no fear of becoming unemployed.''[11] Sometimes ''direct personal observation'' leads to sound conclusions, but sometimes it does not. In this case it does not. Is that sign in an area where unemployed people see it? What about the people who can't read the sign? While the sign says ''Help Wanted,'' do they really mean *experienced* help wanted? Or high school graduate help wanted? Or white help wanted? A sounder conclusion was reached by Economist Robert B. Reich: ''Help-wanted advertising has stayed high even when unemployment rises, indicating a decreasing demand for laid-off workers.''[12]

President Reagan is known to occasionally hold up the ''Help Wanted'' classified advertisements from the Sunday *Washington Post* and assure his listeners that anyone who *really* wants a job can get one. I've looked at those ads. I like to believe I'm a reasonably talented person, but I am not qualified for perhaps 95 percent of the jobs listed. I am not a computer operator or a beautician; I can type, but no one would want to hire me as a secretary; I'm not an engineer or a chef. And what chance does someone have for one of those jobs who can't read and write? What if you can't speak English well? Or at all? What if you have a prison record? What if you have an obvious physical handicap? What if you're a person who is not mentally retarded but close to it? What if you are nervous and you don't make a good impression in an interview? What if you are black or Hispanic or a woman and the employer discriminates, but you can't prove it? I do not suggest that everyone facing unemployment has these handicaps. Most people unemployed are not dramatically different in background from most people who are employed. But using classified ads as a barometer of unemployment is not a good index for unemployment rates, nor for the problems many people have finding jobs.

The lesson some policymakers draw is that it is politically safe to be indifferent to unemployment. They point not only to the U. S. 1984 election, but also to the Thatcher victory when Great Britain had a 12 percent unemployment rate and the Gonzalez victory in Spain when there was a 22 percent jobless level.

What is true politically is that the gravity of what unemployment means to those who face joblessness has not penetrated deeply—nor is there a widely held belief that government action can change the picture much. Inaction is tolerated and the misery is accepted or ignored.

A 1980 study of 127 men measuring forty-two possible life-changing emotional events found loss of job trailing only two other experiences in its emotional intensity: death of a spouse or death of a close family member.[13] A 1983 psychiatric study reached the conclusion that unemployment "has a profound impact on emotional and physical health."[14]

Martin Luther King said, "In our society, it is murder, psychologically, to deprive a man of a job or an income. You are in substance saying to that man that he has no right to exist."[15]

I read recently about a five-year-old getting ready to go with her father to her first day of kindergarten. She asked him to wear a suit so the other children would not think he was unemployed. A five-year-old! What if he had been unemployed? The perceived shame that is part of unemployment is one that is shared by the entire family of the person unemployed, even a five-year-old.

"Small incidents" surface that indicate the unemployment problem is severe for those afflicted. Orland McCafferty, fifty-eight, of Lee's Summit, Missouri, who could not find work, set himself on fire in front of the White House. A few weeks later a small item in the newspapers reported that he had died. On the north side of Chicago, John Pasch, Jr., held an elderly woman hostage after killing his landlord and a police officer. Buried in the end of the story was the fact that he lost his job as a machinist six years ago. Patrick Sherrill worked in the post office at Edmond, Oklahoma. After he was reprimanded by two supervisors and told he might lose his job, he returned to the post office the next morning and killed fourteen people, then shot himself. These are not typical cases, fortunately, but they illustrate the extreme stress that people can go through when they lose a job.

Unemployment figures and the tragedies that go with them hurt the nation in a variety of ways.

They hurt us internationally.

I have been active in pushing the Soviets to permit their citizens married to Americans to join their spouses here, to get the Soviets to permit citizens who want to emigrate to Israel or some other country to do so, and to get them to honor the human rights of their people more generally. I visit the Soviet Union every two or three years, and a standard line of their response to exhortations on the human rights issues is, "You pay more attention to human rights for individuals than we do, and we pay more attention to collective human rights. For you to tolerate all the unemployment that you have in your country shocks us. You are a much wealthier country that we are, but no one in the Soviet Union is ever out of work more than a very short time. We protect our people much better than you do."

I recognize the weakness in their argument because the fact that they provide employment for all their citizens does not excuse their miserable human rights record for individuals. But I acknowledge that their criticism of our tolerance of unemployment has validity. The question I ask myself is: Can our free system devise a way to guarantee a job opportunity for all our citizens? If the Soviet

Union (and soon even China, apparently) can do this for their people, is our free system incapable of doing it?

I come to the conclusion that our free system can do it *if we try and we must try.* We have to make a higher priority of putting our people to work. Why does Japan have an unemployment rate of 2.6 percent, Italy 6.0 percent, Sweden 2.8 percent and Switzerland less than 1 percent when we have unemployment hovering around 7 percent even with our generous-to-the government way of calculating it? The major reason is that these countries have made a priority of putting people to work.

I do not suggest that we put people to work for international public relations, but the political impact of our inaction on the rest of the world is significant. Our relationship with Third World nations depends on many things, but our success—or lack of it—in part depends upon our ability to control unemployment because each of these countries is faced by a substantial unemployment problem. They like to follow good examples. We should be providing them with a better example of how a free system can solve the problem of unemployment.

If we were to expand job opportunities in our society, the Soviets would not suddenly shift their domestic human rights stance, but the effect on many of the developing nations would soon be measurable.

There is a prevailing myth that the Third World view of the military strength of the two superpowers will tip the political scale from one side to the other. But examine the facts: After World War II, the Soviets completely dominated the Warsaw Pact countries, China and, for a period, Indonesia, the fifth most populous nation, as well as Egypt, and the Sudan and other nations. Now China is independent, the Warsaw Pact countries occasionally show streaks of independence—Romania even voting with the United States against the Soviets on the Afghanistan question in the United Nations—and Indonesia, Egypt, the Sudan and other nations once considered completely dominated by the Soviets are no longer considered Soviet puppets by anyone. Soviet influence has risen in Cuba and Nicaragua and a few other countries, but the overall political trend has been a negative one for the Soviets. While their military power, relative to the United States, has grown over the last three decades, their political power has declined.

The United States should maintain a position of military strength, enough to provide a military shield for nations that may need help in protecting themselves; but the day of political allegiance automatically following military power is a day of the past. More significantly, the day when the leaders of developing nations were almost automatically Marxists is a day of the past. The leaders of developing nations are primarily nationalists, interested in taking whatever international political steps will help their countries. The East/West military equation has little to do with their decisions.

The Soviet ability to provide jobs has appeal, no question about it. But these new leaders are not blind to the deficiencies of the Soviet system; they see China trying a modified Marxist system that works better. If we could show them a free system that guaranteed job opportunities for our citizens, that would add considerably to this country's international political appeal.

But the domestic impact of a sensible policy should be our principle motivation.

An opportunity to work gives people self-esteem, something we all need. When self-esteem disappears, alternatives that are not good for society emerge. People without self-esteem cannot convey self-esteem to their children; people without hope cannot give hope to others. After more than three decades of public life and working with people who have every variety of problem, I have learned that the great division in our society is not between black and white, Anglo and Hispanic, Jew and Gentile, or rich and poor. The great division is between those who have hope and those who have given up. There is nothing like a job to raise self-esteem, to feel you are contributing something to society and to your family. For too many in our society, hopelessness and joblessness are the same.

No state or region should feel it is immune to the unemployment problem. For years Texas seemed to enjoy such immunity, but no longer. The Sun Belt states seemed destined to have endless growth, but now ten of these nineteen states have unemployment rates above the national average.

Feelings of helplessness in the face of unemployment are fed by the "conventional wisdom" now being passed along to younger people: You will be the first generation of Americans that will not have it better than your parents. That conventional wisdom could turn out to be correct, but only because we permit it to be. It is not inevitable, but that downward trend in expectations has an impact on the jobless, their fears and hopelessness.

Desperation and frustration and a feeling of uselessness are not the only costs. There is also the staggering economic loss to the nation of having millions of non-productive people who could be productive. That loss is well over $160 billion annually.

When the Bureau of Labor Statistics announced in January, 1986, that unemployment had fallen (temporarily) to 6.6 percent, the *New York Times* editorialized: "Willing workers who can't find jobs are an expensive waste, and none are more wasted than the young trying to get started. Two of every five jobless workers in January were under 25. The unemployment rate of black teenagers increased in January 41.9 percent; the rate for black college graduates under 25 hovers near 17 percent, compared with less than 5 percent for whites." The editorial called for action against the "unsolved problems of economic waste and human misery."[16]

When we fail to provide employment, the costs reach far beyond the jobless.

In Peoria, Illinois, Caterpillar employed 32,770 people in 1980 but only 18,000 in 1985. That one company purchased $418 million in supplies from firms within a fifty-mile radius in 1980, $300 million in 1985. Real estate taxes paid in the three immediate counties dropped one million dollars over that same period. The value of homes plummeted. How many people in grocery stores and clothing shops and car dealerships and hardware stores lost their jobs as a result of the Caterpillar layoffs? No one knows. Thanks to hard work and good leadership, I sense that Peoria and Caterpillar are starting to rebound. But in the meantime, thousands of people have been hurt.

While the depression in sectors of the agricultural economy is not the same as unemployment, its economic impact beyond those immediately hit causes unemployment. In four years, employment at agriculture-dependent International Harvester (now Navistar) dropped from 97,000 to 15,000. Small towns are devastated by the agricultural slump. (The agricultural tragedy in the nation is a significant problem, but one that requires much more extensive treatment than I can give it in this book.) The havoc of unemployment is more visible in a small community, but the economic suffering is felt in any community where there is joblessness, even though it is less dramatically visible than it is in Peoria and small communities.

Not surprisingly, areas of high unemployment are also areas of high crime. The cost of crime in economic terms is huge. The cost of crime in agony to the victims is even greater. By tolerating unemployment and the resultant poverty, we also tolerate a discouragingly high crime rate. One of every 40 black men born in the United States will be murdered; one of every 131 white men will be murdered. For women the statistics are better but not good. Three years before his death, Martin Luther King said, "Hopeless Negroes in the grip of rage will hurt themselves to hurt others in a desperate quest for justice."[17] No one suggests that unemployment is the sole cause of crime. But neither does any serious student of the problems of crime suggest that joblessness is not a major feeder of crime.

Rockford, Illinois, is in many ways a typical American city of medium size (population 139,712), but a community that until recently had significantly above average income. The economic recession of the early 1980s, together with a depression in the machine tool industry, sent incomes plummeting and unemployment skyrocketing. The author of a comprehensive study of a new phenomenon in Rockford, youth gangs, wrote: "Rockford unemployment has been the single most contributive factor in the rise of youth gangs, youth offenders, and youth-at-risk."[18] Unemployed youth want money, and if they have no alternative, crime is too often the obvious answer. Unemployed youth have time on their hands and abundant energy, and when a job does not demand that time and energy, something else will. Sometimes they choose crime. During the past six years there has been both national population growth and growth in the total number of jobs, but the number of full-time jobs held by teenagers has dropped almost 30 percent, a major cause of crime.

Children who grow up in families where no one works do not learn basic attitudes and work habits that are essential to performing effectively in our society. In a real sense unemployment can be "inherited."

The cost of joblessness in family breakups and child abuse is overwhelming. A 1964 study noted: "We [came] upon remarkably strong correlations between unemployment and all manner of family dysfunction. The percentage of married women separated from their husbands was then recorded each March. This was compared with the male unemployment rate of the previous month, for the years 1953-64 (the period during which both statistical series had existed). A correlation of .73 appeared. This suggested to an analyst that changes in unemployment rates might account for as much as half (i.e., the square of .73) of the changes in separation rates. At four months the correlation was .81, suggesting that as much as two-thirds of one set of changes could be accounted for by the other. Correlations this strong are known to social science but are not common."[19]

A book about "the plight of poor women in affluent America" reaches the conclusion that in addition to a widespread need for jobs for women, a fundamental force in the destabilization of the American family is male unemployment.[20]

Teenage pregnancy is a major problem for the nation. It is particularly severe in areas of high unemployment. Some view the phenomenon as primarily a problem in the black community. Not so. In economically depressed southern Illinois, for example, teen pregnancy rates are high in all-white counties with high unemployment figures. Nationally, 11.5 percent of all pregnancies are teenage pregnancies. In almost all-white southern Illinois counties where jobs are scarce, teenage pregnancy rates soar: Pope County, 18.5 percent; White County, 18.9 percent; and Hardin County, 21.0 percent. In southern Illinois counties with a large black population the figures are even higher (as is unemployment): Alexander County, 23.8 percent; Pulaski County, 24.5 percent.

The largest newspaper in the area did a story on teen pregnancy and had this insightful observation from one young mother: "Candace thought having a baby would give her the chance for the only job she saw available in her impoverished hometown: motherhood."[21] A mother of two, she and her children live on the $324 a month she receives from welfare.

If this country is serious about the continuous cycle of teen pregnancy and poverty, we had better provide more constructive alternatives than pregnancy. Show me an area of high unemployment, and I will show you an area with high teenage pregnancy rates.

Reporter Leon Dash of the *Washington Post* lived for seventeen months in a depressed area of the District of Columbia called Washington Highlands. After writing a six-part series on teenage pregnancy and seeing the grimness of the lives of those involved, he reflected on its significance, and among his conclusions: "As I reported the series, I realized that teenage pregnancy was tied to self-esteem which in turn was tied to work. I reached a point where I could tell, when I walked into anyone's house, who was working and who was not by the expression on a person's face. If they were happy I knew they were working. The unemployed and recently laid off were always sullen. . . . I began to think about how many of us middle-class professionals take our jobs and our careers for granted. We don't recognize how much it fulfills us in terms of self-esteem. A lot of the negative behavior I saw and was told about I came to see as being intricately linked with a person's ability to earn an income."[22]

The suicide rate among the unemployed is higher than among

the employed. When Vandalia, Illinois (population 6,000), lost jobs, the unemployment rate was not the only thing that grew, according to an Associated Press story. There were six suicides in six months, "an unusually high rate; mental illness cases jumped 35 percent, and requests for help for alcoholism increased 137 percent."[23]

Illness increases among those out of work for three reasons: lower nutritional levels, less willingness and ability to get medical care until problems become severe, and the tendency of both the mind and body to respond more favorably to activity than to inactivity. Alexander, the great Macedonian king, knew that when he said, "Those who labor sleep more sweetly and soundly than those who are labored for."[24] Unemployment leads to poverty and poverty leads to illness. In early eighteenth century London, where the poor concentrated as their one last hope, three out of five boys died before the age of sixteen, a statistic that shocks us. But we tolerate less dramatic statistics and assume their same inevitability as Londoners did two centuries ago.

Mental illness is higher among the unemployed than among those working.

The nation is becoming more sensitive to the problem of homelessness on our city streets. Why are they homeless? One recent study says, "Loss of jobs is the major reason."[25]

Discrimination is more of a problem for minorities and the handicapped and women when employment is down. Lift employment, and the scars and wounds of discrimination start to disappear.

A study by Professor Harvey Brenner of Johns Hopkins University found that a 1 percent increase in unemployment caused a 5.7 percent increase in homicides, a 4.1 percent increase in suicides, a 4.0 percent increase in prison admissions, and a 3.5 percent increase in mental hospital admissions. While there may be dispute on the accuracy of some of these precise statistics, it is difficult to disagree with the observation of William W. Winpisinger, international president of the Machinists Union, about the statistics: "The plain fact is that unemployment kills."[26]

A 1986 survey of disabled persons by the Louis Harris pollsters showed that 80 percent of those disabled and working were satisfied with life, but only 62 percent of those not working found satisfaction in life.[27]

Drug use is high in many of the areas of joblessness.

Alcoholism is higher among the unemployed, ironically among the people who can least afford money for drinking.

Unemployment often hits rural areas first. As it penetrates there, the least skilled—who tend to be the unemployed—in their desperation move into urban areas, compounding the problems of the cities. In 1959, the central cities had 27 percent of the nation's poor; by 1983 that had grown to 36.5 percent. Yet in 1983, a smaller percentage of the nation's total population lived in central cities, making those poverty statistics even more dramatic.

In May 1975, more than two-thirds of those unemployed were drawing unemployment compensation benefits. By October, 1985, only one out of four officially listed as unemployed was drawing unemployment compensation benefits. Life has become more severe for the jobless.

The most dramatic unemployment figures are among young people, but perhaps those most distressed by being out of work are those in the forty-five and older age group who have worked for a company twenty or twenty-five years and suddenly find themselves out of work. Finding a job at that age is not easy, and pride is hurt in addition to the economic hurt. Older workers tend to be out of work longer.

Business is harmed by unemployment. People who are not working do not buy new cars or air conditioners or suits. Tax incentives to stimulate business investment *sometimes* can be effective, but creating an economic climate in which people are working and buying *always* stimulates the economy.

The federal budget suffers. President Reagan uses the figure that one million people unemployed costs the federal government $28 billion. Others in his administration use the figure $35 billion. Let's be conservative and say that the federal expenditure for food stamps, welfare, unemployment compensation, Medicaid and a host of other expenditures—plus loss of revenue—amounts to $25 billion for each one million unemployed. If we had programs that reduced the numbers of those unemployed from ten million to five million, the net savings to the federal government would be $125 billion, using the most conservative figure. Cutting unemployment in half would also result in a growth of our gross national product of at least 4 percent, or approximately $700 for every man, woman and child in the nation. *What a tremendous economic loss we suffer through our indifferent acceptance of high unemployment!*

Even that great financial impact is not as important as the psychological cost. Three thousand years ago, Solomon told us: "There is nothing better, than that a man should rejoice in his own work."[28] Three centuries before Christ, Aristotle wrote: "The happy life is thought to be virtuous; a virtuous life requires exertion."[29] And two hundred years before that, the famed lawmaker Solon warned, "An abundance of laborers should not be left idle."[30] Plato wrote, "A State is not one, but two States, the one of poor, the other of rich men; and they are living on the same spot and always conspiring against one another."[31] Machiavelli said much the same thing. To the extent that a government can avoid hopelessness among the poor—and reduce the number of the poor—the two states can become one state.

Those who are unemployed feel left out of society. They do not have a feeling of contributing, of belonging. Yes, they can vote, but in a very real sense, they feel disenfranchised. There is a growing sense among them that their voice is not being heard.

Cynicism grows. We cannot have an increasing number of people who feel alienated from their system of government without having a loss of national spirit. It cannot be measured, but that loss is there. When that cynicism and loss of national pride and spirit combines with other factors—such as the assassination of Martin Luther King—you have an explosive situation. Employed America is blissfully unaware of the powder keg on which it is comfortably seated.

William L. Deadmond, a labor leader in an area of high unemployment, wrote me that he has had "to explain to my son and daughter why the American dream is slipping beyond their grasp."[32] What happens to the spirit of this country when parents feel compelled to tell that to their children?

It is difficult to argue with the heading of a *Chicago Sun-Times* editorial: "Jobless Rate: A Disgrace."[33]

Ironically, at the very time that unemployment has crept up, the average welfare payment has dropped, a decline that averaged 33 percent for a family of four between 1970 and 1985. The poverty rate among our citizens is the highest it has been since 1965. Between 1975 and 1982, there was an increase of more than 50 percent in those under the age of sixty-five living below the poverty level in New York City. The children suffer most. Nationally, after some years of drop in poverty rates among children, this rich nation that continues to produce nuclear warheads endlessly—after we can already destroy the earth thirteen times with them—now has one-fourth of its preschool children and one-fifth of its school-aged children living below the poverty level. In 1984, this nation had 33.7 million people living below the poverty line, eleven and one-half million of them children below the age of fifteen. Of the 1983 statistics, Senator Moynihan observed: "For the first time since the federal government began keeping track, there was a simultaneous increase in wealth and poverty within the population."[34] While the percentage living below the poverty line climbed during the first years of the Reagan Administration, the sales of Jaguar automobiles tripled. Poor and unemployed people may not know all of these statistics, but they understand the reality. They are frustrated. It is the function of a political system to show them a non-explosive way of solving their problems.

The heading on a front-page story of the *New York Times* (March 16, 1986) summarized the situation in five words: "Millions Bypassed as Economy Soars." *U. S. News and World Report* had a cover story about the healthy, solid growth in the economy, but buried in the story was this sentence: "Companies are laying off employees, forcing unions to give back wage gains, closing mar-

ginal plants [and] shifting more production overseas.''[35] *A polit-*
ical system that has a ''healthy'' economy with more and more
people not sharing in its prosperity is headed for trouble. Where
that trouble may lead, no one knows, but no one can be sanguine
that his or her comfortable nest will be untouched.

Thomas Winship, a former editor of the *Boston Globe,* wrote:
''The press is missing the biggest domestic time-bomb story of
the decade. . .the worsening plight of the underclass in our large
cities. . . . The depressing fact is that real poverty in the United
States has been increasing at the same time as prosperity is increasing for the upper half of society. . . . We [the press] simply
are not examining with adequate vigor the broad rising problems
of the poor, much less exploring avenues of possible solutions.''[36]

Almost a decade ago when the employment picture was rosier,
the Committee for Economic Development, made up of some of
the most prominent business leaders of the nation, expressed concern: ''We believe that this country must make a strong national
commitment to high employment and to a situation in which the
number of job openings essentially matches the number of those
seeking jobs at reasonable wages and in which people able and
willing to work have adequate opportunities to be trained and
guided toward suitable job vacancies within a reasonable period
of time.''[37]

That awkward sentence was true when written in 1977, and its
truth is even more pressing today.

They added, ''We believe that this country cannot justifiably
deny its citizens the opportunity to work for an adequate income
and to be free from the desperation and frustration that frequent
or long-term unemployment can bring.''[38] Far more Americans
are out of work today than when that statement was issued.

It should surprise no one to have the president of the Chicago
Urban League, James W. Compton, urge: ''We must lobby Congress to pass a national full-employment bill so that every able-
bodied American citizen may be gainfully employed.''[39]

There was a time when few Americans worried about drugs.

It seemed a distant problem faced by people in some other section of a city or state. But its evil tentacles gradually reached out to touch every neighborhood in the nation.

Like drugs, unemployment is still distant from most Americans, but its drumbeat is getting louder, and its consequences will gradually spread to every neighborhood and home in the nation.

The time to stop its growth is now. The leader in that effort must be the federal government, working with the private sector. Pressing national problems rarely, if ever, are solved by national inactivity. Certainly a national open wound the size of our unemployment problem will not be healed by pious speeches about free enterprise or dismissing the depth and nature of the inflamed wound by suggesting that local and state governments have the ability to handle it. A festering wound the size of our unemployment problem will only grow worse through inattention. The private sector can help and should be given more encouragement to help. State and local governments also can offer assistance. But without national governmental leadership our problems will worsen. Without creative, practical, compassionate answers, the human resources of this rich, marvelous country will not be used to help these people and to help our nation become more productive and competitive. And we will be less able to help the rest of the world.

In a series of articles on the nation's poor, *Chicago Tribune* reporter Timothy J. McNulty wrote: "Politicians, black and white, generally have been too timid to face the problem of the underclass or even to recognize it publicly."[40]

Unfortunately, he is right, but politicians are not alone in their indifference. Novelist Harry Mark Petrakis was describing each of us a little when he wrote, "In the midst of multitudes we exist like barricaded islands, fearful or unwilling to reveal ourselves or to discover the meaning of others."[41]

In chapter 4, I outline what can become the key to moving away from the result of that insularity and indifference, a Guaranteed Job Opportunity Program. But before that, in the next chapter, I want you to meet some unemployed people so that you have a better sense of who they really are and what their struggle is. Then, in chapter 3, I spell out some basic steps that should be taken to strengthen our economy, to build a better foundation for the Guaranteed Job Opportunity Program.

If your reading takes you no further than this chapter, remember: *We have an urgent, potentially explosive unemployment situation that will not be resolved without action.* Whether that action is positive and constructive—or is destructive—is yet to be determined.

Endnotes

1. Daniel Patrick Moynihan, *Family and Nation* (New York: Harcourt Brace Jovanovich, 1986), p.22.

2. President's Commission on Industrial Competitiveness, *Global Competition, The New Reality* (Washington: Government Printing Office, 1985), Vol. 1, p. 1.

3. Bruce R. Scott and George C. Lodge, *U.S. Competitiveness in the World Economy,* Working Paper (Boston: Division of Research, Harvard Business School, 1984), pp. 1-2.

4. Courtney Burton, Jr., Chairman of the Board of Oglebay Norton, *Congressional Record,* Dec. 12, 1985, p. S 17477.

5. Lester Thurow, *The Zero-Sum Solution* (New York: Simon and Schuster, 1985), p. 23.

6. *Ibid,* p. 47.

7. Richard Fox, *Reinhold Niebuhr, A Biography* (New York: Pantheon Books, 1985), p. 269.

8. Testimony of Dr. Leon H. Keyserling, House Subcommittee on Employment Opportunities, Sept. 4, 1985.

9. Office of Technology Assessment, *Technology and Structural Unemployment: Reemploying Displaced Adults* (Washington: Government Printing Office, 1985), p. 34.

10. Cynthia Marano, Executive Director, Wider Opportunities for Women, before the Senate Labor and Human Resources Committee, Apr. 30, 1986, unpublished.

11. Herbert Stein, "Still at Work on Full Employment," *Wall Street Journal,* Feb. 13, 1986.

12. Robert B. Reich, *The Next American Frontier* (New York: Times Books, 1983), p. 202.

13. "Simplified Scaling for Life Change Event" by Richard H. Rahe, David H. Ryman and Harold W. Ward, *Journal of Human Stress,* Dec. 1980.

14. "The Relationship Between Job Loss and Physical and Mental Illness" by Duane Q. Hagen, *Hospital and Community Psychiatry,* May 1983.

15. Coretta Scott King (Ed.), *The Words of Martin Luther King, Jr.* (New York: Newmarket Press, 1983), p. 45.

16. Editorial "What's a Low Unemployment Rate?", *New York Times* Feb. 14, 1986.

17. Martin Luther King, Jr., speech in Westchester County, New York, quoted in Moynihan, *op. cit.,* p. 39.

18. Webbs Norman, executive director of the Rockford Park District, letter to Paul Simon, Mar. 11, 1986.

19. Daniel Patrick Moynihan, *Family and Nation* (New York: Harcourt Brace Jovanovich, 1986), pp. 22-23.

20. Ruth Sidel, *Women and Children Last* (New York: Viking, 1986).

21. Elizabeth Renshaw, "Candace: 'As long as we can get by...' " *Southern Illinoisan,* Mar. 10, 1986.

22. Leon Dash, "Young Black Pregnancies: Truth is the First Answer," *Washington Post,* Feb. 9, 1986.

23. "Vandalia's Revival Hasn't Developed," Associated Press, *Southern Illinoisan* (Carbondale, IL), Apr. 21, 1986.

24. Alexander the Great, quoted in *The Lives of the Noble Grecians and Romans,* by Plutarch, *Great Books of the Western World* (Chicago: Encyclopedia Britannica, 1952), Vol. 14, p. 560.

25. Milton Meltzer, *Poverty in America* (New York: William Morrow, 1986), p. 22.

26. William W. Winpisinger, *Let's Rebuild America* (Washington: Kelly Press, 1984), p. 48.

27. Louis Harris and Associates, Inc., *Disabled Americans' Self Perceptions,* survey conducted for the International Center for the Disabled, p. 40 of the summary.

28. *Ecclesiastes* 3:22, King James Version.

29. Aristotle, *Nicomachean Ethics,* Book X, Chapter 6, quoted in *Great Books of the Western World, The Works of Aristotle,* Volume II (Chicago: Encyclopedia Britannica, 1952) p. 431.

30. Solon, quoted by Plutarch, *The Lives of the Noble Grecians and Romans, Great Books of the Western World* (Chicago: Encyclopedia Britannica, 1952), p. 72.

31. Plato, *The Republic,* Book VIII, *Great Books of the Western World* (Chicago: Encyclopedia Britannica, 1952), p. 406.

32. William L. Deadmond, letter to Paul Simon, Jan. 20, 1986. (Mr. Deadmond is a leader of the United Auto Workers Local 434 in East Moline, IL.)

33. *Chicago Sun-Times,* Dec. 22, 1985, p. 27.

34. (Moynihan) p. 110.

35. "Brave New Economy," *U. S. News and World Report,* Mar. 31, 1986, p. 46.

36. Thomas Winship, "Disciplined Intelligence: An Effective Weapon for Social Justice," *Nieman Reports,* Winter 1985.

37. John L. Burns et al, *Jobs for the Hard-to-Employ* (New York and Washington: Committee for Economic Development, 1978), p. 12.

38. *Jobs for the Hard-To-Employ, A Statement on National Policy* (New York: Committee for Economic Development, 1978), p. 15.

39. "We Must Save Black Families" by James W. Compton, *Chicago Tribune,* Feb. 25, 1986.

40. Timothy J. McNulty, "Roots of Underclass Found in Racism, Failed Policies," *Chicago Tribune,* Sept. 16, 1985.

41. Harry Mark Petrakis, *Stelmark* (New York: David McKay, 1970) p. 110.

Chapter Two

The People

THE STATEMENTS in this chapter have been chosen not because they are dramatic—though each is in its own way— but because they are typical. As you read through these stories, real stories of real people, you will find that the skeletal frame of unemployment takes on flesh and blood, it becomes more than an abstract statistic. How were these people selected? When I heard about someone who was unemployed, I asked his or her permission to tell the story. That's why many of them are from Illinois. I met three of the men whose stories are included here through the work-release program of the District of Columbia corrections people. In Baltimore, Congressman Parren Mitchell and I went outside of his office onto the street, and he quickly found unemployed people. Each story is different, yet each is the same. These people are not saints. Some are people you would not want to hire if you were an employer. Two of them did not make a good impression in their interview; the rest did. But people who do not make a good initial impression are also people who need jobs. One or two may arouse your antagonism rather than your sympathy. After reading these accounts you will understand the dimensions of unemployment a little more. There is a common bond among these people who do not know each other—a bond of frustration, lack of self-worth, discouragement and, at times, hopelessness. These are not carefully screened stories intended to give dramatic impact, but the stories, reduced in size, of the first twenty-eight people I encountered after launching this book. It is important that you listen to all twenty-eight. Each story is an individual reminder of failure, and in large part that failure is a national failure. One truth will hit you. All unemployment is personal.

Donald Ruyle

*Donald Ruyle, thirty-three, lives at Rural Route
2, Gillespie, Illinois. He and his wife have one
son. His wife worked one day last year, and has
worked two or three months in the last five
years. She is a member of a union in Carlinville,
Illinois. He worked at the Fiat-Allis plant in
Springfield and was laid off four years ago.
Shortly after that the plant closed.*

I'VE LOOKED ALL OVER and there's just no work.
I've been trying to get on at a refinery, and they was supposed
to let me come in for an interview, and then the refinery caught
fire and that did away with that job possibility altogether.

I've been places and stood in line five hours, four-and-a-half
hours another time, but no luck. I talked to my wife and said I
had to relocate. The United Auto Workers had a telephone we
could use to call anywhere in the United States. I called down South
and to other states, and all I could get were jobs paying $3.35
an hour. By the time you move your family down there and got
a house and tried to make a living, it would just be impossible.
Fortunately, my wife and I have been saving up for almost ten
years to buy a house. In the four years since I lost my job, I've

worked about four months on construction work. That's it. I've been dipping in pretty heavy into the money we saved up for our house, which we ain't going to get, I guess.

You hear of jobs opening and get your hopes all filled up and by the time you get there, you find out they're not hiring or the jobs are filled. I don't know, I just don't have no confidence in myself any more. I'm thinking that there should be a way, you know, that the United States should be able to put their people back to work.

My thirteen-year-old son don't get to do the things that other kids do if their parents are working. That bothers him a little. I try to explain to him that we've got to use every bit of our money that we've got for necessities. Sometimes my wife and I get nervous and upset, but being out of work hasn't bothered our family life as much as some families I know. We haven't seen a movie in the four years I've been out of work. We've stayed home the last four years. We've been trying to watch our money carefully. When I look to the future, I'm afraid my son is gonna have a hell of a time, excuse the language.

Right now I'd be happy to get a minimum wage job, particularly if it had health insurance. I wouldn't be setting here worrying about if my son got hurt or something and he was in the hospital. I told my wife that if one of us got sick and had to go to the hospital, that'd be the end for us.   □

Lynette Davis

Lynette Davis, twenty-one, is a high school
graduate, is single and has no children. She
lives in Baltimore.

I HAVEN'T WORKED for two years. I'm looking for
any kind of work. I've been to the post office, to different stores.
I go to the unemployment office and look at their job chart.

Some day I'd like to have my own business, maybe a beauty
shop.

Not having a job is depressing. You're not able to have money
to buy the things you want and need. Like clothes.

But when you're a woman and you're black and you've had leukemia, people don't want to hire you. I stopped taking my chemo-
therapy several months ago. My leukemia is in remission. But they
use all kinds of excuses. We couldn't hire you because you might
have a relapse. I went to the supermarket, Foodarama. I had filled
out a job application, and when they called me for a job inter-

view, you know, that's when I told them about my leukemia and everything. And they said no I think it's best that you don't work here because there's so many chemicals and things around. My doctor says I can work. And I could work a cash register.

If you finally get an interview, they say we'll get back to you. Then you never hear from 'em. You go through the Sunday ads in the papers, but as soon as you call them on Monday, they say the position is filled.

I hope I get lucky and find something.   □

Gerald Yusko

Gerald Yusko, fifty-two, is married and has five children, three of them still living at home. He lives in Streator, Illinois.

I WORKED TWELVE YEARS at Owens Illinois Glass and then lost my job because of automation. Automation and so many plastic bottles instead of the more expensive glass bottles. I've been out of work a year and a half. I get a little part-time work in at a food processing plant in Streator, and once every three months or so I may get in a full week. I was getting $9.02 an hour in my full-time work, and now I'm getting $6.71 an hour for the few hours I get in. My wife does not work. It's tough. In the close to thirty years I've been married, I've never been unemployed until now. I worked for a company that made sewer pipes that closed down, but I was off less than a week before I had the Owens Illinois job. . . . When you find yourself out of work, you get a case of nerves or something. You get sick to your stomach; you just get depressed. You know, you don't even hardly enjoy being with your family because you got this on your mind all the time.

I've tried everything to get a job. I've been to the six different Job Services offices in the area. I'm eligible for Job Training Partnership Act program right now, but you've got to have employers to be able to get the job, and they like to get the people that, say if they need a welder, somebody that's already welded before. So they get the job. They want the people that's already trained really.

The thing that's saved me is that I have my house paid for. The only lucky thing about all this is that I happened to get my home paid for before all this happened. Otherwise I would have lost my home.

I worry about my children. Unless I get steady work, I won't be able to further their education after they get out of high school, if I can get 'em through high school.

I worry a lot. Being out of a job, I've got that on my mind constantly. You shouldn't let it prey on your mind constantly, but I've got a habit of doing that. Sometimes you get so nervous, you know, you figure you just can't go on anymore.   □

John Hill

*John Hill, twenty-nine, lives in Washington,
D.C. He is married and has four children.*

I LET SOMEBODY use my car who got involved in
a burglary. They came to my house and got me. I was accessory
to the fact. So I got 180 days in this half-way house. They let me
go out during the day now and look for work. Every time you
ask for a job, they say come back in one or two days or that they'll
notify you. But they never notify you and the job's never there.
If they know you've been locked up, you don't have a chance.

I got to the twelfth grade, but then there were family problems,
and I didn't graduate. That doesn't help.

My wife works at a cleaners. She makes a little better than $150
a week, but rent is $210 a month and then you have to pay for
electricity and gas. I got four teeny kids. My oldest is eleven. They
need shoes, clothes, everything. The two oldest are getting more

clothes-sensitive. If it wouldn't be for my mother helping us a little, we'd really be down. We've already been on the verge of losing our place twice because we couldn't pay the $210 rent. We don't get welfare, food stamps, nothing.

It's causing family problems. She's always telling me I wish you'd get a job. She don't think I'm trying.

Being out of work makes you bitter. You can't help your kids. I'd like to take 'em somewhere on weekends. I can't buy 'em nothing. Even when the ice cream truck comes by, I can't give them nothing. I feel disgusted. It makes me just feel like I don't have anything to offer.

I'd take any kind of a job. Minimum wage would be great. I'd sweep the streets, pick up trash, remodel houses.   □

James Metcalf

James Metcalf, fifty-three, lives in the Chicago suburb of Hanover Park. Married, he has three children ages twenty-three, twenty-two and sixteen. The oldest is in the Air Force, and the twenty-two-year-old just graduated from Western Illinois University.

WHEN I WAS ON THE FARM near Homerville, Ohio, I had dreams of working with electronics. I was drafted into the Army in 1956, and was trained in electronics. In 1960, I joined IBM. I was trained to repair and maintain many different machines. I also installed equipment in manufacturing plants. This was far beyond my wildest dreams.

I was an electronics technician. I worked for several different companies, but the last company had to lay off most of their employees in September of 1984. I've never been unemployed before. My loss of job came up quite suddenly. I went to a consulting firm, and they helped me with my resume and gave me a list of industries related to my profession. I sent out almost sixty resumes. I had one interview. I've been answering the ads in the papers, trying other consulting firms in other states. They'd always give me some excuse or another. I tell ya, if you're over forty, it's almost impossible to get a job. They'd rather hire somebody out of tech school or a recent college graduate.

I've tried everything. I studied real estate sales—that took about ten weeks. I applied for my test in October and got my license in January. I've been tryin' to sell real estate, and in the meantime I've taken tests for the Postal Service. But there you have thousands of people applying for only a few jobs. I've been able to get some temporary jobs, working two or three days at a time.

Fortunately, my wife works for the local school district. But we've had to cash in our life insurance. We had some CDs, but we cashed them in to make the house payments and to pay the utilities. But that's just about gone now.

Being unemployed is something like having an operation. You really feel the effects of it. If it's somebody else, well you see the guy and then you go on with your own business until it hits you. Then it's permanent. There's no waking up from that dream. And with all my education and background, you would think I could get a job.

I had to retrain myself. I was fortunate enough that I had some help. But some people don't have any technical training.

When you're out of work, you really need somebody that shows a little concern. It doesn't take much to give a "Good morning" or a "Good afternoon," and when you're really down, that means a lot. I've gone to Catholic Services, the Protestant ministers, private organizations to get help on getting a job. They're all tryin' to help. It's so important that we help each other.

When I could not get work, my sixteen-year-old daughter couldn't comprehend how she could go on to college. She even talked about suicide. We had a talk with her, and I think we got it settled. And she's doing well now, carrying about a 3.5 average. I'm proud of her; the whole family is.

I was born and raised on a farm, and either we work or we don't eat. That's how we was trained. Farmers are struggling now, and I'm struggling now. I guess that's born into you. You just try to keep going. You have failure after failure. You try to keep going. It's very discouraging. It's really frustrating.   □

Lisa Thies

Lisa Thies, twenty-five, has a master's degree in college student personnel work. She suffers from osteogenesis imperfecta, a disease sometimes referred to as "brittle bone disease." Her bones have gradually strengthened and are less of a problem than when she was a child. She is shorter than most people and is confined to a wheelchair. She is married. Her husband works in the box office at a Washington, D.C., theater.

My LAST JOB ENDED ten months ago. I was working in Indiana, but there were some family problems, and my husband and I decided to move to the Washington area. Before we left, however, we had an automobile accident, complicating our lives. When we got out here, I really thought I would probably find a job before my husband did. With my two college degrees—he has one—I thought I'd probably get a job first.

Just getting by is difficult. Right now we're staying with a friend of mine from college in a one-bedroom apartment. With three people and our dog we brought with us, we're kind of cramped in that small apartment.

I get a small Social Security disability check, and my husband has a small income, but we're trying to still pay for the van and things like that. It's tough.

Because I'm drawing disability, if I could get a job, the federal government would be saving some money. I've passed around the federal government personnel form and my resume like it's confetti. I've taken the clerk typist test, and that seems to have sparked a little interest, but for someone with a master's degree to settle for a clerk typist job is discouraging. I'm frustrated at this point because I feel I'm going to have to settle for something to get money coming in because I can't find anything that needs my qualifications.

One of the things that most people don't understand is that not working not only hurts you financially, it hurts you psychologically, also. Not having a reliable wheelchair made it harder for me because I couldn't really get out and look for a job. I needed a reliable wheelchair to get out and look for a job, but I needed a job to pay for a reliable wheelchair. I had days when I felt I was just a burden to everyone. You wonder how you got into that position and how you can get out of it. And when I talk to people about a job, I'm either not qualified because I don't have enough experience, or I'm over-qualified because of my schooling.

I also got frustrated hearing people say, "Well, I don't have anything, but let me refer you to . . ." That was fine at the beginning. I'd go and meet the other people, but after three months of that and no results, you just get sick of hearing that.

I ended up going to the Vocational Rehabilitation office here in Virginia. They helped, but they're slow. It took them seven months to get me a new wheelchair. They didn't call Indiana for any of my past files. They made me go through all the requalifying exams again. That was a waste of time. It wasted two months.

At this point, I've received a few calls for clerk typist interviews. So maybe something will work out for a job, even if it's a job I don't want forever. I'd really like to find something in my career area.

But they see me, a female in a wheelchair, and they think secretary. That seems to be the immediate reaction. It makes me want to throttle them right there. Females, whether in or out of chairs, aren't necessarily secretaries.   □

Jon Bierman

Jon Bierman, forty-five, is married and has one college-age son. He lives in Peoria, Illinois.

I WORKED IN THE MARKETING department at Caterpillar. Our department was in the midst of reorganization. I knew that my division would be relocated and I'd probably be reassigned. I knew somehow I'd be affected, but I didn't have even the remotest idea that I'd be affected in the way I was. In fact, my boss on two different occasions assured me that I would not be affected other than relocated. They just called me in one afternoon, and this guy says, "We've had this reorganization going on here. We're trying to figure out where we're going to put various people and you don't fit. Therefore, we're going to terminate you." I worked two more days and then took my vacation time.

I've been out of work almost a year now. I was shocked when they let me know. Absolutely shocked. Hurt.

I have a degree in marketing and everyone said, "Well, you're in great shape. You can go off and find a job in marketing anyplace." I knew the product line I specialized in perhaps better than almost anybody else in the company. Unfortunately, there isn't a great deal of demand for someone with my specialized knowledge in my field. I was making $60,000. Now when I tell someone what I was making when they are looking for someone for $30,000 to $40,000, you scare 'em. When you tell somebody what you were making, they're thinking that even if they give you a job at 50 percent of your former salary that you'd never be happy because you're used to living on a lot more money. So they don't even make an offer.

I've had one job in nineteen years. . .and it's not just the money either. It's being busy and feeling like you're doing something.

My wife works as a dental hygienist, but this has hurt her, too.

I send my resume to dozens of ads in the *Wall Street Journal* and other publications each week. That's produced two responses. I am calling twenty to thirty companies each week. I'm just pulling my hair out just sitting here trying to land a position and eager to get started on a new one.

Fortunately, I was able to financially prepare myself for what I thought would be a good, secure retirement some day. I use my reserves to live on now.

Other guys have a really tough time if they're in their early fifties. If I were thirty-five, getting another job would be a snap. Forty-five is difficult. But if I were fifty-five, it would be impossible.   □

Maria Garcia

Maria Garcia, thirty-two, has three children,
ages eight, six and five. She lives in Chicago.

I HAVE BEEN OUT OF WORK for seven years. I worked for three or four months for a Chicago company but they fired me. My son was sick, and I took him to the doctor, and they gave me permission [to be absent] for one day. The next day I had to take him again, and I called the company, but the secretary was not there and they don't take the message. I was absent three days, and when I go back, they told me I didn't have a job any more.

I receive $385 a month from welfare and pay $200 a month for my apartment. I also get $250 a month food stamps, but it's never enough.

As a woman living without a husband, I am afraid someone will try to break in my house. I don't have a telephone to call for help. I cannot afford one.

One of my sons does not learn quickly. In kindergarten when he needed special help, there was never any available. He then went to first grade and had to repeat it. He is now in second grade when he should be in third. And he will have to repeat second grade next year. He is finally being sent to, how do you say, special classes. We live near Harrison Park, and my boys are in the swimming team and all the children on the team have to have good grades or else they are taken off the team, and my son was taken off the team. He was the only one taken off the team. Every day he goes to swimming, but he doesn't go inside the pool. He only looks. He takes his book to write so they can see he can learn. But really he can't. He hasn't learned in four years; he won't learn in two months.

To help my son who needs special help, and to get a telephone, I need to work. I don't want to be on welfare. You get lazy. I want to learn something, to get a job so my children are not raised as they are now.

At the medical clinic they ask you how you pay the rent and the light bill. In front of everyone, they make you feel as if you are the very low. And that you are lying. I have heard them say at the clinic, "These people always say the same thing."

I am fighting to find a job. I want to work. I have taken training, and I want to work. I need to learn how to speak better English.

I buy clothes in a second-hand shop. The kids are growing and they want better clothes. They always see the difference in their friends. Welfare is not enough. I want to work and I cannot. The lack of experience and the lack of English hurts me. I can answer the phone, but I cannot have a long conversation.

I have another problem. My children were all born with crooked legs and they need special shoes. They are expensive; they cost $25 to $30 a pair. I cannot buy them for all three so I buy the one that is needed the most.   □

William George

William George is nineteen and a high school dropout. He lives in Baltimore.

I LEFT SCHOOL in the eleventh grade because of family difficulties. My mother and three sisters at home was having a tough time. I wanted to help them. I've been out of work six months. But I've never had a full-time job. I just get a little here, maybe a dollar there to help take care of me and my people.

I've been applying at different places. They're supposed to call me back but they never do. I've just wasted my time doing that. I'd like to get a job as a janitor someplace. I look through the want ads, but there's never anything suitable for me. The fact that I haven't had a full-time job makes it tougher to get one. They don't want to hire someone who hasn't worked full-time.

My mother can't work. She needs help with my sisters.

Sometimes I dream about having a job, coming home to a nice family in a nice home. But that's just dreaming.   □

Mathias Rodgers

Mathias Rodgers, forty-eight, is married and has five children. He lives in Clinton, Illinois.

I SERVED IN THE ARMY for eight-and-a-half years. In Vietnam, I received a wound to my foot, and shrapnel in my right side punctured my kidney. I'm still suffering from that, but the Veterans Administration says that it's less than 10 percent so I don't get any disability pay. But I lost a kidney and also had a brain tumor removed caused by a skull fracture I had in the service.

My last full-time job was with General Electric in Bloomington. Then they reduced their force, and I lost my job. I got a job for seasonal work at the grain elevator in Weldon last November. My wife works at the Eureka Company in Bloomington and makes just enough so that we don't draw any welfare. My unemployment compensation ran out.

It's getting to be tough. The oldest of our five children is fifteen, the youngest, five.

You wouldn't believe what I've done to try to get a job. I've gone all over Illinois and to other states. I've written at least 200 applications and sent resumes. I've heard all kinds of excuses from employers. You wouldn't believe them. Either you're overqualified or underqualified or you wouldn't be satisfied with the pay or this or that or something else. But you know they're not telling you the truth.

When you see people working, doing things, and you can't do them, it really hurts. Especially it causes a lot of tension in the family. They don't understand it because you're so used to gettin' what they want.

I'm gonna be honest with you. My children look down on me pretty hard because their mother's doing all the work and I'm not doin' nothin'. They think I've failed. Every once in a awhile I get slam remarks like, "Well, what's the difference; you're not working, you're just freeloading." It hurts, it really deeply hurts. The situation has gotten so bad at times that we've been on the verge of divorce.

I've got myself into several training programs to get better jobs, but things just don't work out. The jobs aren't there. There's times you just wonder what you're gonna do. I get so disappointed. I've been refused jobs because at the age of forty-eight, I'm too old. That's a fact. I know they're not supposed to do that, but they do it.

Before I got laid off, my wife and I used to enjoy dancing once in awhile. We don't do that anymore. I've even forgot how to dance almost.   ☐

Mr. Rodgers was sent a copy of the interview to make any possible corrections. He responded and included this sentence: "By the time you get this letter, my wife will have divorced me."

Laura Akhla

Laura Akhla, forty-three, was born in Baghdad, Iraq, and is Assyrian by background. She has a fifteen-year-old son.

I WENT TO SCHOOL in Iraq, an American school, and worked for the American Embassy for six years until the embassy was closed down. I had to leave the country, simply because I went to an American school and worked for the American Embassy.

I had an arranged marriage to someone in Kuwait. It shouldn't have happened to me because of my background, American schools and modern parents, and I knew that he wasn't the right person for me. After four or five years, I told the charge d'affairs in Kuwait, who used to be my boss in Baghdad, that I just couldn't take it anymore.

I came to the United States in 1974, and shortly after that applied for a divorce.

But getting a job is not easy. I have so much knowledge in that part of the world that there must be companies, like Standard Oil, that could use me in their foreign affairs department. I want an income, I want to live, I want my son to have a good education. They look at me, and the fact that I'm a woman, and they say to themselves, "How much can she do for us in that part of the world?" I've had contractual jobs, the last one a two-year contract. Since that finished, I decided to do my own freelance work, translating. But it's been difficult. My former boss has taken me back for part-time work because he wants to help me. But it's part-time work, paying five dollars an hour.

It's hard to break through with these large corporations. Maybe it's my resume.

I'm a hard worker, but I haven't been given a chance.

I know computer in both languages. I have an administrative background. I like learning.

The Presbyterian Church has really helped me. They have also helped my son. He has been great through all of this. A person of "Catholic interests" has affected our lives greatly.

I want growth for both of us, the growth opportunity that I did not have when I was married. It was just horrible. When I was making good money, before the oil glut, I gave him the opportunity to have more, culturally. I took him to the theater and musical things. But for the past eight years, I just couldn't.

I'm not looking for money. I'm looking for quality of life.□

Arthur Payton

*Arthur Payton, twenty-five, lives in Washington,
D.C., and is single.*

COLLEGE STUDENTS can get the jobs. I didn't
graduate from high school, but all I need is one more point to pass
my GED. I left high school because I had a chance to work hanging dry wall and plastering.

But now it's tough because I've been locked up for fifteen days.
They don't care what kind of record you got, but if you've been
locked up, it's hard for people to trust you. I saw these two guys
coming at me, and I knew they were going to jump me so I hit
them first. I got in a fight. They gave me ninety days, but I was
in jail only fifteen days.

One of the reasons they don't want to hire you if you've been
in jail is they think: drugs. A lot of people get into jail because
of drugs and there's drugs in jail, too. That makes it tough for
someone like me who's been in jail and not on drugs.

I worked at a car wash once, and if I could get a job like that
back again, I would. You gotta start somewhere.   □

Charles Slaybough

*Charles Slaybough, thirty-six, is married and has
two children, ages eleven and sixteen. He lives
in Mounds, Illinois.*

I'VE BEEN OUT OF WORK three years, though last
year I worked for a month on construction work. I was a building
maintenance employee and worked for ten years straight on that
job. I never figured I'd have a problem. Then the layoffs came.
At first you're surprised. Uh, bewildered. You've got security
when you've got a job. You know that your check's coming in,
you support your family, not the greatest in the world, but you're
able to support 'em. Anybody that's earned their own living feels
responsible for themselves. It's a good feeling. I never thought
I'd be out of work three years. I keep looking, and I keep trying,
but being unemployed for such a long time, you become deeply
depressed. I'll be honest with you. The depression sets in. You
can only take so many denials. You figure the whole world's just

closed in on you. And I'm becoming more unemployable as each year passes by. People don't like to hire someone who's been out of work three years.

I was making $1,825 a month plus a free apartment. Now I draw $309 a month, plus $223 in food stamps and have to pay for my housing. Now I'm costing the state money instead of paying taxes.

Last summer I got a job for three weeks. I put in every minute I could and got in a lot of overtime. I worked fourteen- and fifteen- and sixteen-hour days. I grossed $1,400 and took home about a thousand dollars after deductions. When I notified the welfare office, they deducted my full $1,400. I lost $400 by going to work. That doesn't give me an incentive to go out and find a job unless it's full-time and permanent.

My sixteen-year-old daughter has a chance for part-time work, but that gets deducted from our welfare also. There's no incentive.

Being out of work creates extreme pressure on the household. Not working you don't feel like a man. And it's hard to discipline your children in the proper manner. I'm not talkin' about physically disciplining them, just normal discipline. They say to me, "Well, you're not working, Daddy, how can you tell me what to do?" It creates a lot of conflict in the house, and then you feel inadequate. Then your wife has a problem because she's not gettin' the funds she actually needs to run the household. Then you start drinking, then after drinking you're just deeper and deeper. And then you have fights with your family and your wife. Then you're back to the depression again, and the depression's even three times worse this time. Probably 30 to 40 percent of the people who are hanging around bars here are unemployed.

My children's school work is affected. My daughter has failing grades, though my son is doing well. I've tried to help her but it's difficult.

We don't have money for anything. No movies. I can't even afford a haircut. I cut my son's hair, and my wife cuts my hair. I don't even smoke anymore.

If they took the money from welfare and put people to work,

I'd at least have a chance for advancement. And I'd feel better about myself.

My wife's looking for work, too, but it's awful discouraging.

My dream is to some day have a job and a new car. I'm thirty-six-years-old, and I've never had a new car in my life. □

Ruben Gonzalez

Ruben Gonzalez, twenty-three, is married and has three children, ages four, three and one. He lives in Chicago.

I WAS BORN IN BROOKLYN, New York. My father was born in Cuba, and my mother was born in Puerto Rico.

I dropped out of Lincoln Park High School in my senior year. I've worked at a lot of different places since then. The one I worked at the longest was for Quick Pak, delivering items. I worked there about four months. I was paid minimum wage, $3.35 an hour. Once I had a job at Work Bench and got $200 every week. Now I'm on welfare and work at jobs where they send me to keep my welfare. But I've never had a job long enough to collect unemployment. I get laid off. A supervisor or foreman tells me I'm not doing my work right.

They ought to raise the minimum wage a little. At $3.35 an hour with a wife and three children, it's hard.

I want to get my high school equivalency, GED.

Welfare covers health insurance for my children, but for my wife and me, it doesn't cover hardly anything. I got a cut on my hand, and I couldn't even get generic so I just used regular aspirin.

I've been looking for work for four months. I would love to work. I would love to have a job and support my family. With three small children my wife can't work. Sometimes we need food, and there's no money, and she says to me, "Why don't you go out and find this, look at this, see if you can find an application and try and find a job." But when you go, they tell you they will call you, and they don't call you at all.

I'd like to have a job so that I could save money on the side for an emergency. Or maybe even for travel.   □

Herbert Rice

*Herbert Rice, twenty-two, is single and lives in
Springfield, Illinois.*

I HAVEN'T BEEN OUT OF WORK for too long, according to a lot of people, but three months is long for me as far as my bills and car payments and everything like that. They've already turned off my telephone. And I have ulcers now. As far as social life goes, that is kind of difficult to be going any place and trying to enjoy yourself when there's little money to spend. In addition to getting a job, I'd like to go back to school and get a degree in business administration. There's a lot of people my age that's out there on the street now. They claim they haven't given up, but I see them out there doing things that will put them in no place but jail.   □

Willie Morris

Willie Morris, twenty-eight, is single and lives in Chicago. He graduated from Kennedy-King Junior College and unsuccessfully tried out for professional baseball.

I'D LIKE A JOB in the business field with an opportunity to grow in the business. At times I get very depressed. But when I get depressed, I just continue to pray and just let God take care of it. There must be a reason for this. When you're out of work, you get no respect from people. If I had a job, it'd be different. I stay with my mother, and I'm really not even supporting myself. She has five kids to support plus me, a grown man. It's tough on her, and she can't feed all of us. Just this past week I struggled as far as eating. I took two days without eating, really without letting her know because I didn't want to put any more pressure on her. Then when I do eat, I try to buy bread and peanut butter just to get by. □

Robert Bertrang

Robert Bertrang, thirty-one, is single and lives in Springfield, Illinois. He is blind.

I'VE BEEN OUT OF WORK since January of 1982. I'm an eighth grade graduate, but in 1976, I took a course in medical terminology and medical translation at Lincoln Land Community College. I spent eleven months at the Illinois Visually Handicapped Institute in Chicago. While I was in Chicago, I took a job playing piano at a restaurant and bar combination up there. I did that for about four weeks, and then I finally said, "That's enough. I'm heading for home where I can be with my family and friends." In addition to job problems, I've had some inner ear and ulcer problems. I'd like to get a job as a switchboard operator or as a receptionist. I really want to earn my own living. Disabled people get tired of being shoved into sheltered workshops.   □

Barbara Payne

Barbara Payne, thirty-seven, is a divorced mother of three children, ages seventeen, fourteen and seven. She lives in Baltimore.

I'M ABOUT TO GRADUATE from Sojourner Douglas College, a private black college. They have good teachers there. And then I want to go to graduate work in the School of Social Work at the University of Maryland. I want to be able to help people.

I've been out of work five months, and that means you're not able to afford the things that you want. I do receive child support from my husband through the Department of Social Services, but if I want to get a refrigerator on credit, when I put on the credit application that I'm only getting that once-a-month check, they won't accept the credit application.

With three kids, it takes so much to support three kids. You have school supplies to buy, tennnis shoes, jeans. And food stamps don't provide enough to take care of a family. For my three children I get just over a hundred dollars. It's not enough to get the nutrition they need—the right vitamins to make their bones strong and just to make them healthy, period. If they're not getting the right nutrition, then they're not going to be healthy brain-wise or any other way. And they're not going to function well in school. And other pressures affect kids, too. Sometimes kids don't want to go to school if they have holes in their shoes.

Now that I've just graduated from college, I have my application in at several places, and I've taken some tests. I'm at the top of the test list for one job.

Being black is a problem in some places, not all. It's not as bad as it used to be. Being a woman is a problem. You don't make as much as a man. Maybe ten years from now that will change. Women now have to take jobs they don't want to take, like bus drivers. They take those jobs, and those jobs aren't really good for most females. They end up with a lot of health problems.

But the job market is very bad, particularly for teenagers. My seventeen-year-old boy has a learning disability. He's not eligible for any disability assistance, but people take advantage of him. They take advantage of the weak. If somehow I could be sure the seventeen-year-old could have a job, I'd feel better about the future.

□

Ed Heyer

Ed Heyer, forty-eight, is married and has three children. He lives in Cicero, Illinois.

I WAS LAID OFF at General Electric Hotpoint in November, 1981, when they cut back because of lack of work. If my wife weren't working as a secretary, we'd be out in the street. I was making $9.25 an hour and had insurance coverage when I was laid off. Being the so-called breadwinner of the family, I've lost my self-respect, lost my dignity. My spirits have not been high to say the least. Emotionally I've been very down and thought about doing a lot of stupid things, like wanting to jump off a bridge.

Your family, after awhile, they say well, when are you going to find a job; we need money, we got a ton of bills, how are we going to pay them? My fifteen-year-old son is not able to get the kind of clothes he needs or participate in student activities like he'd like. He likes to play baseball, but he hasn't done it for two years because the registration fee is thirty-five or forty dollars.□

Leota Johnson

*Leota Johnson, middle-aged, is single and
supports her mother. She lives in Chicago.*

I'VE BEEN OUT OF WORK three-and-one-half years
out of the last five years. I'm a machinist, and I was making twelve
to thirteen dollars an hour. My unemployment ran out last year.
If you got a little too much, you can't get welfare. My mother
and I live in an apartment that rents for over $400 a month. Then
you're talking about food and electricity and gas and all the basic
things of life. I went after a job, and they told me if I got an "A"
on the test, I had a good chance getting the job. I got an "A,"
and everything went fine, but then they tell me they have only
one job. It's got to the point if you don't know nobody, you won't
get in. Unemployment is not only bad for those of us out of work,
my cousins who have jobs are worried about losing their jobs.
When the President gets on television and talks about people not
being hungry and plenty of work out there, I wish he would write

me personally and tell me where it's at. Being out of work—I could see people doing away with themselves out of fear. You grow up comfortably to my age, and all of a sudden, everything starts coming at you financially, and you can't handle it. It's frightening because you don't know what the outcome's going to be. I even start eating food that I hadn't eaten in twenty years. Seriously. I hadn't eaten a neck bone or pig's feet since I entered high school. I don't know what I'd do if I had a really big family. My mother's eighty-seven, and she's never been out on the street, but she doesn't know how close we are to being there. Emotionally, it tears you down.□

Thomas Williams

Thomas Williams, forty-five, is single and lives with his mother in LaSalle, Illinois.

I'M DEPENDENT ON MY MOTHER for my room and board. I make my own health insurance payments out of savings I have. But now I've been out of work six-and-one-half years. I worked as a construction laborer. Factories put out notices that they're not hiring. And it's hard to get a job even like dishwasher in a restaurant. If you don't have experience, they're not interested.

Being out of work depresses you. I've lost a lot of personal esteem, as far as doing something in the mainstream of your home society. You don't fit in. In the last five years, I've been following every possible want ad, as far as janitorial work goes, either for a part-time job or a full-time job. But I don't get much response. I might get one or two calls a year through the Job Service. I've been thinking about going to Chicago to see if I might be able to get a job like at a service station. But my mother lives alone here. I hate to leave her, and right now I'm even more dependent on her than she is on me. ☐

Eddie Smith

Eddie Smith, thirty-three, lives in Washington, D.C. He is not married but is trying to help support his twin daughters who are fourteen.

I WAS BORN IN GREENVILLE, South Carolina, and came to Washington when I was eleven. I went to school to the tenth grade but then quit to help my mother. She had five kids to raise. My father left her when I was very young. I wanted to get out and help her. Not finishing high school has hurt me. But I feel you shouldn't be knocked out of a job because you didn't complete high school. You should be given a chance.

I was in jail on an assault charge, got out, and I was doin' all right. I had a job, was reunited with my family. But they said I violated my parole, and I had to go back for eight months. I came back from Occoquan and now I'm tryin' to get back on track. The job I had before I went back to prison paid between $6.00 and $6.50 an hour. When I got back, my employer wouldn't give me my job back. He didn't say why but it was this parole thing. Then I got another construction job that lasted about five weeks until that job was finished. Since then I've been out of work but I'm looking constantly.

No, I didn't finish high school during my eight years in prison. Sometimes you let pride stand in the way of gettin' what you should. I learn a little slower than others. But I'm a great mechanic, and I can do construction work. But if you don't have the schooling to go with it, it's hard to get a job.

I'm not married. I wanted to marry at a young age, but I didn't have much education, and I didn't think it was right. But I've tried to help with the twins I'm father to. When I was down at Lorton Penitentiary, I made something like $119 a month. I would send half of that money home for them. I was tryin' to do the best I could even though it wasn't much.

I have about $600 worth of carpentry tools, but I just can't find the work. It's frustrating, but I'm taking one day at a time because I know that God is with me 'specially if I keep Him out front. I know how frustrating this must be for my family. You just gotta take one day at a time. ☐

Carolina Garcia

*Carolina Garcia, forty, lives in Chicago. She
and her husband have four children, the oldest
fourteen, the youngest seven.*

I STUDIED OFFICE WORK in two schools in Mexico,
but I didn't work at it. I'm now studying office work at SER Jobs
for Progress, a Chicago-based job training program. I worked for
five years in a restaurant as a waitress and then children began
to come and so I could not continue to work.

My husband cannot work because he has developed heart problems. We are on welfare now. We get $450 a month in cash plus
food stamps for six of us. My husband did not work long enough
to draw Social Security disability.

I don't want to go back to working as a waitress. I didn't like
it much. People said very bad things. I want to work at something
that does not make me feel so bad.

I was born in Mexico, but we are legal immigrants. Three of

my children were born here. We like this country, but I want to work. Out of the $450 welfare we get, we must pay $200 for rent, plus gas and electricity and telephone. We have a telephone. We had a child die who was two months old of cardiac problems. We did not have a telephone then.

I have always wanted to go to a school where they teach us how to speak English, where the teacher is interested in our learning. You have to learn to speak the English language. It is the most important thing.

I want my children to go to college, to become doctors or engineers or something like that.

I want to work at anything, even if it is not an office because it is difficult for me to speak English. I want to work at a place where I can learn English. Going to school has been good for me. I am not so afraid, and I speak more English and understand more, but it is still not enough. I want to learn everything so that I will not wonder what is being said.

I would like to work for a company where they would give me an opportunity. Some day, I would like to work in an office and earn good money and buy the kids everything they need.   □

Greg Johnson

Greg Johnson, thirty-eight, is divorced but supports his twelve-year-old son. He lives in Springfield, Illinois.

I'VE BEEN LAX in supporting my son lately because I no longer have a job, and I've run out of my unemployment [compensation]. The Urban League has been trying real hard to come up with some position for me.

I had a job as a consultant for a weatherization project in Arizona. By the time I got there, they had fired the director, and my job was pffft. I decided rather than being sixteen hundred miles away, I'd come back. I had a six-month contract in Colorado, and I got it completed in three and a half months. They probably would've hired me, but every time I would call and talk to my son, it'd be "Dad, Dad," so I came back to be with him.

I've been running into the same question whenever I go for an [state job] interview. First they ask do I know anyone, and second, there seems to be a little form, it's a yellow form, that has to be filled out by the Republican Committeeman and signed by the Republican County Chairman before you can be hired. Since I never voted Republican, there's no way that I could show them that I was an avid Republican.

I've gone on interviews and had the director or whoever was interviewing me tell me that he was very impressed with my qualifications, and then they look on the back of the paper to see if there are any initials. You have to have initials from Republican leaders that I didn't have. There were several positions in state government that I applied for that they just came out and asked me did I have any political support. I said no, I'm just tremendously qualified for this job, and I never heard another thing. It gets a little depressing.

I have A's on state tests for approximately twenty-five state job titles. I do get a token interview, in part because I'm also a veteran, but after you've been on so many interviews, you can tell. . . . I have good references, my job performance and just general attitude. I just want a fair shake. I went to school nights and Saturdays for fourteen years to get my bachelor's degree.

I've been to Hardee's and Wendy's, and they say I'm overqualified. I think their rationale is that if a position does come along that pays more money that I would like, I'd leave. Which is probably the truth.

My twelve-year-old worries about me being out of work, worries a lot. So does my mother. Being out of work is hard on me, too. I have too much time. I'd like to be doing something constructive with my mind and my hands. Just sitting around, trying to scrounge an interview, just so you can fill in the form to get your unemployment or whatever is just bluh. Your self-esteem deteriorates. My grandma prays for me that I can get a job. She turned ninety this March, a grand old lady.

It takes a very strong relationship to hold a marriage together if you're unemployed. It's very hard on a person, not only the person unemployed but the people in his or her immediate circle.

I've made several mistakes in my life, big ones. And I'm paying for them. I'm an ex-con. I've been out fourteen years. On the employment forms it doesn't make any difference if you've been convicted last week or fifty years ago. You have to check "yes" and explain.   □

Terry White

Terry White, twenty-five, is a high school drop-out, but he is wearing a high school ring and a Georgetown University sweatshirt. He is single.

I'VE BEEN OUT OF WORK four years. Without being a high school graduate, you don't get a job. I'm getting by doing odd jobs for my uncle.

I was working at McDonald's, but then the manager and me didn't get along. And since then, I've just been looking for jobs.

I'm mailing an application for a hotel/motel management school. I'm working on my high school equivalency tests now.

I live with my mom. She gets on my back every morning. She tells me to go out there and look for a job. And that's what I've been doing. You've just got to take one day at a time, 'cause it's hard. Particularly if you haven't finished high school. And I didn't drop out, I got pushed out. If I don't pass my GED test, I'll study some more and just go back again.

I love beautiful things. Sometimes I think I ought to just go out and knock somebody out for the money. But I don't do that. I've just got to get work.

I've got a nine-year-old brother who needs help, too.

I'm studying hard. I know I can do it. And I've just got to take one day at a time and let the Lord take care of things.   □

Jose Vazquez

Jose Vazquez, twenty-four, lives in Chicago with his parents. He is not married.

WHEN WE FIRST ARRIVED HERE, of my four brothers and my four sisters and my parents, only one brother spoke English. Whenever there was a medical problem, we didn't know what to do. I have an enlarged heart, and I have migraine headaches and asthma.

For a long time when my father made a low salary and had a large family, we did not know there were programs like food stamps that we were qualified for. The problem my father always encountered whenever he looked for help was a lack of interpreters. He speaks a little English but at times he gets confused and will say something meaning something else.

I want to work and study at the same time. I am studying office skills now because that will help me get a job, but then I want to study engineering. I want to save money and help my family.

My father was a migrant laborer and then learned the trade of butcher. Now he works in a meat packing company in South Chicago, and he makes a good salary and supports the entire family. But the job has its disadvantages, like the cold. He is old and cannot take it. If my dad cannot continue to work at the meat packing company, what can he work at?

I have urged my brothers and sisters to study. I told my sister who graduated from high school that if she earned a "B" average, I would buy her a car. I tried to motivate her. She earned a "B" average, but I do not have the money to buy her a car.

After finishing studying air conditioning in junior college, I went looking for a job. I tried many places all over Chicago. They want five years of experience. If no one gives me an opportunity, I am never going to get experience.   □

Freeman Pickens

*Freeman Pickens is twenty-nine years old and
lives in Washington, D.C. He is single.*

I'VE BEEN IN RETAIL SALES, mostly men's clothes
and men's and ladies' shoes. And carpentry. I would prefer carpentry, more money. But if I ran across a job right now that paid
minimum wage, I'd take it. If you want to go higher, you have
to start at some point that's going to be lower.

I'm better off than a lot of people. They can't fill out job applications even. If you can't fill out the job application, no man's
gonna hire you. If I'm having a hard time getting a job, you can
imagine what it's like for the guy who can't fill out a job application form.   □

Doris Longworth

*Doris Longworth, thirty-two, is single. She lives
in Chicago.*

I WENT TO LAWRENCE UNIVERSITY in Wisconsin and
majored in anthropology. And then I went into public relations.
(Laughs.) I got a job doing public relations for a medical association. After some time I was promoted to newsletter editor. When
a new boss was appointed, she made it known to me from very
early on that she did not see eye-to-eye with me at all. So I left
the organization a year ago. I haven't been working since. I was
fired. The woman was treating me like garbage. And that's not
just paranoia speaking. It was recognized by others in the organization before I left.

After I was fired, I needed a kind of period of therapy and relax-
ation. I thought, well, the summer's here, and I'll just do some
thinking about what direction I want to go. Then in August we

had a family tragedy. My sister suddenly died of a stroke. That knocked me out for a couple of months. Since then I've just sort of been sitting back. I'm just terrified that once I make a move, I'll end up in the same situation again. Monday I'm going to see a woman who specializes in job counseling.

Being unemployed has been awful. I was on unemployment compensation for awhile. I've had help from my parents. Economically it was difficult, and there is also a whole lot of anxiety. I had car payments to make and other living costs. But more than that, I was stuck in this whole mindset. I thought I really can't do anything. Maybe the woman I didn't get along with was right. Maybe no one will ever want to hire me again. . . . This whole idea of going through job interviews and having to recount this story bothers me. Now I've been unemployed for a year, and people wonder what the hell I've been doing. Try to explain that. It's been really difficult.

When I was working, I was used to this whole routine. You know, dress like this in the morning. Now I don't have this routine, and I'm single. I think for a lot of single people, work is like a second family. And then that's all grabbed away. I remember the night after my last day of working at my job, I went to dinner in Greektown with two dear friends of mine, women, and in the middle of the meal I suddenly turned to them and said, "I just realized that I don't know what I'm going to do when I get up on Monday morning. I have no idea."

If I had started looking for a job right away, I'd be in much better shape today.

The woman I worked for has since been fired. But I still have self-doubts. Sometimes I think I must be totally incompetent, and yet I know better. Being single and out of work is bad. But if I had three kids to support, it would have been horrible. I just can't imagine how horrible it would have been. □

THE TRAGEDY OF THESE STORIES is that they are all unnecessary. These people need not suffer because of unemployment. Life has enough difficulties and burdens without the added weight of being without a job, without the added weight of feeling useless, without the added sense of being a burden to your family. Unemployment is not an affliction from God but an unintended result of flawed governmental policies. And when we improve those policies, it is not only the unemployed who benefit but all of us, through a richer, fuller, more efficient and productive economy. Unfortunately, the unemployed are generally not the people who influence policy. It is essential that those comfortably employed rouse themselves to speak up for people who too often are politically voiceless.

It is also essential that we recognize that we can change this increasingly grim picture. This nation can be competitive; we can innovate; we can be more productive; we can avoid the tragedy of joblessness you have just observed in twenty-eight people who represent ten million others.

The other day I asked someone on my staff to set up a dinner "think-tank session" on how we can move toward an inexpensive means of converting salt water to fresh water. It is a change that would dramatically improve the standard of living for hundreds of millions around the globe. After consulting with a few "experts," she came back and told me that they said it is not possible. I told her to get some other experts, that the question is not whether it is possible, it is only when it will be done. We had our dinner, and we are working on this potential.

The question on stopping unemployment is not whether it can be done, it is only when it will be done. Unfortunately the naysayers are with us in the employment field as in every other area. U. S. economist Robert R. Nathan outlined for the South Korean government the economic path that country should follow to economic growth, an outline that resulted in dramatic growth for South Korea's economy. (Unfortunately, the South Koreans did not follow his recommendation to maintain a stable democracy.) About the U. S. economy, Nathan writes: "Unfortunately too many economists are beginning to resign themselves to substantial unemployment as inevitable and therefore the acceptance of higher and higher rates as a manifestation of full employment. Instead of trying to find solutions to this waste and idleness, there is a tendency to look on the recent unemployment as somehow being inevitable...that we're always going to have more unemployment than in the past. If present tendencies persist, it won't be too long before some analysts will regard 10 percent unemployment as acceptable and that 90 percent employment means full employment."[1]

Robert R. Nathan is correct. Those who assure us that we cannot have full employment are the spiritual heirs of the scientists who said that human beings could never fly and that the idea of transmitting pictures into a television screen was an utter impossibility.

Full employment in a competitive and productive America can and must become part of this nation's future. It is clearly achievable. The only question is how many people must suffer needlessly before we act.

Endnotes

1. Robert R. Nathan, letter to Paul Simon, July 15, 1986.

SECTION TWO

SOME ANSWERS

Chapter Three

Our Economy:
The Broad Sweep

Iᴎ ᴏɴᴇ ᴏꜰ ʜɪꜱ ꜰɪᴠᴇ-ᴍɪɴᴜᴛᴇ ʀᴀᴅɪᴏ addresses to the
nation, President Reagan had a line of early-year admonition to
make 1986 "a year to unite for full employment, from Harlem
to Hawaii, so that every American who seeks work can find
work."[1] Fine words, but we need more than fine words.

Putting people to work is not going to be accomplished through
some sudden, single, dramatic move. Creating the right kind of
tomorrow is much like creating a mosaic, with a host of small
pieces, all essential to the final picture.

As conservatives and liberals work together to create that mosaic,
they will be surprised at how much they agree.

In this chapter, I discuss some things that can be done—and a
few that are being done—to alleviate unemployment and to en-

courage a more competitive, productive nation. In the following chapter, I discuss a fundamentally different approach that can undergird and make possible the next major breakthrough for an improved society: Guarantee a job opportunity to every American.

The bulk of the new jobs will continue to be provided by the private sector, and expansion of the private sector should be encouraged, particularly in ways that make the United States more competitive and productive. But, however adequately we stimulate private sector employment, the reality is that we will continue to need public sector leadership if we want to avoid drifting into a situation in which more and more of our citizens are unemployed.

In 1978, the Committee for Economic Development stated: "We believe that this country must make a strong national commitment to high employment and to a situation in which the number of job openings essentially matches the number of those seeking jobs...."[2] To achieve that laudable goal requires private and public sector cooperation and leadership.

Action by the federal government is essential as a base for an effective jobs program in these broad areas: fiscal policy, trade policy, and education and training policy. These areas are also essential to accelerate the growth rate in productivity and to enhance our international competitiveness. Without improvement in policy in these three areas, any jobs legislation will help but will not be as effective nor as fully attainable as it should be. Without action on these three fronts, an effective jobs program also will be much more expensive. Movement on any of these items helps; action on all is essential to have a really effective assault on the unemployment problem.

Fiscal Policy

Most Americans are not aware that our basically sound economy is sliding onto very thin ice. They do not see the connection between imprudent fiscal policy and high unemployment. For fiscal year 1987, the expenditure for interest by the federal government will be approximately $207 billion. The administration provides a smaller figure of $149 billion, but that is deceptive. The administration figure is the *net interest* figure. They subtract the sum earned by Social Security trust funds, for example, from the total interest expenditure. The $207 billion figure is the one that should be used.

That $207 billion is:

—More than 20 percent of the federal budget.
—More than half of the total individual income tax paid.

While in Fiscal Year 1962, for the first time we had a total federal budget of more than $100 billion, now we are spending $207 billion for interest alone.

This huge interest expenditure has grown to be the number three spending item for the federal government, only behind defense and Social Security. If current spending trends continue, by Fiscal Year 1991, interest could be number one.

Roughly 60 percent of the huge annual deficit is now financed directly and indirectly by people from other countries, a source that could dry up suddenly and cause us major economic damage and even greater employment problems.

In four short years the United States has gone from being the number one creditor nation in the world to being the number one debtor nation. If we were to have another serious Savings and Loan problem in one of our states, or the closing of a large number of rural banks in Iowa and Nebraska, or some other blip on our economic EKG, there is the real possibility that there would be international "dumping" on U. S. securities, creating major problems.

Between Fiscal Years 1980 and 1986, these were the major growth areas for federal spending, in outlays:

Defense 88%

Entitlements (such as Social Security) 56%

Non-defense discretionary items 20%

Interest 240%

Some believe that we have reached the point where the federal government's interest expenditures will double every four or five years. We cannot continue that for a long period without having the entire economic house crumble.

Conservatives and liberals and those between differ on many things. But there should be no differing on the fact that we have a major problem on our hands. If we want to spend money for programs, we must tax ourselves for them. If we are unwilling to tax ourselves for the programs, then they have to be curtailed or dropped. There is no sensible alternative to facing that reality. Failure to face reality means more money for interest rather than programs, including programs that put people to work. High interest rates caused by deficits discourage construction and capital investment that stimulate employment and make the United States more competitive and productive.

For the last three decades, under both Democratic and Republican administrations, we slowly drifted in the wrong direction. Although we are one of the lowest taxed societies in the industrial world—which is contrary to the public myth—political leaders of both parties have been reluctant to face the decision of either providing more revenue or curtailing growing services. So slowly the deficit grew. And grows. We got deep into the fiscal quicksand with the passage of the tax bill of 1981. It was offered by President Reagan in good faith, and accepted by Democrats, as well as Republicans. People presented him with the theory that you could spend more and reduce taxes, and the stimulation from the reduced taxes would produce additional revenue. He bought the concept. He assured Congress in a special message that if we passed this 1981 tax bill, by Fiscal Year 1984 we would have a balanced budget. He was $200 billion wrong. By fiscal year 1986, the deficit reached $230 billion, three times as high for one year as the deficit of any previous president. The pressure to vote for the 1981 tax bill was immense, because so many special interest groups benefited. It passed both houses of Congress overwhelmingly, with Democrats, as well as Republicans, supporting it in large numbers. It turned out to be a disaster. (I voted against it and against the almost-as-bad competing Democratic package. I wish all my votes were as good.)

If we can start to extricate ourselves from this fiscal mess, the economy will respond favorably. A rough projection is that for each $50 billion the deficit is reduced, the prime rate of interest will drop one percent. That will do three things: 1) It will stimulate construction, automobile purchasing, and other interest-sensitive endeavors; 2) It will cause the value of the dollar to drop on the international market, increasing U. S. exports and jobs, and reducing imports into our country; and 3) It will save the federal government roughly $20 billion in interest payments.

There is no popular way of gradually reducing our deficit. But we have no choice; we have to do it. As we reduce the deficit and solve our fiscal problems, the Federal Reserve Board can adjust so that interest rates will be lower, benefiting everyone.

Part of our present difficulty has been caused by a simple thing that superficially sounds good: We have elected members of the House and Senate who have done what the voters want. When first elected to the state legislature in Illinois, I received a letter from a man in South Roxana, Illinois, who had thirteen points he wanted enacted. The first twelve were increased services he wanted from government, and the thirteenth point was: Cut taxes. That man accurately reflected public opinion, although it is usually not so clear in its inconsistency. *We have fundamentally adopted his program—increase services and cut taxes.* Now we are paying for our folly in lost jobs, loss of national competitiveness, and a massive waste of tax money on interest. Pulling ourselves out of this fiscal mess will be costly but nowhere near as costly as continuing the present course.

In 1986, Congress passed the Gramm-Rudman-Hollings bill, a measure establishing specific targets over a multi-year period to force reduced deficits and eventually no deficit. For Fiscal Year 1987, for example, the target is a deficit reduced to $144 billion. If that target is not met, then there will be across-the-board cuts in almost all programs to achieve that target. Probably no one in Congress favors across-the-board cuts in drug enforcement and defense, food stamps, the FBI, and Federal Aviation Administration inspections of airplanes, as a few examples. But across-the-board penalties force Congress, and people who lobby Congress, to pay attention to the overall fiscal picture, not simply come to Washington with requests for more and more money.

Passage of the Gramm-Rudman-Hollings measure could have two results if Congress sticks with it: 1) We gradually will be forced to reduce the deficit through additional revenue; and 2) We will be forced to stop the wasteful habit of buying every ridiculous weapons system that anyone advocates. The President does not agree that will be the result, but almost all members of Congress of both political parties privately agree, if not publicly.

Those of us who favor greater federal leadership on jobs, health research and delivery, education, and other programs must support the revenue in asking for the appropriations. "Pay-as-you-go" must become more than a slogan. It must become a reality of our governmental life.

In speaking of Gramm-Rudman-Hollings, there are those who say, "Let's get rid of the deficit, but not this way." I notice, first, that most of them have not proposed *any* way of getting rid of the deficit. Where is their program? Instead of hand-wringing about the adverse effects of Gramm-Rudman-Hollings, the hand-wringers should be proposing constructive alternatives. The Fiscal Year 1987 budgets proposed by the Democratic House and Republican Senate under the Gramm-Rudman-Hollings targets do not call for any across-the-board cuts. They are based on reduction in the rate of growth in defense spending, modest increases in revenue, and slight growth in social programs. While these budget changes are opposed by the White House (which does not have veto power over a budget) and the budgets are far from perfect from the perspective of any of us, they are not bad. Similar proposals and remedies will be needed for the next four years until we are finally in control of our fiscal situation again.

One intriguing question is how people who classify themselves as liberals and groups like labor unions—who usually support good causes—can find themselves vehemently opposed to proposals that would reduce the deficit and ultimately create more jobs. Those who represent working people end up defending a fiscal policy that massively redistributes wealth, taking money from hard-working men and women and transferring it to those who are more prosperous. Who pays the $207 billion in interest? Who receives the $207 billion? Working men and women pay the bulk of the money, and those who are economically more fortunate are the major recipients. Senator Dale Bumpers of Arkansas calls this the most massive redistribution of wealth in the history of nations, and as a reader of history, I can think of no parallel. What we are doing is so brazen it would make a feudal lord blush.

Deficits rob from people of limited income in another way. They force up interest rates. People who have to borrow to buy a car or a refrigerator end up paying more; those who lend the money get added income. As interest rates escalate, jobs disappear. Money spent on financing a deficit also robs the federal government of an ability to respond on education programs, health research and assistance, jobs programs, help to the poor in other countries, and other needs. Instead of meeting these needs, we take money from the people who struggle to get by and provide subsidies to the wealthy.

Why do those who generally fight to protect the poor remain silent at this great economic injustice? My sense is that in the days when Franklin D. Roosevelt ran small deficits to get the nation rolling during the Great Depression, those who fought for the poor found themselves fending off the people who criticized FDR for the deficits. They got into the habit of defending deficits. What was a necessary small deficit half a century ago has shifted into becoming an unnecessary huge deficit. But the old pattern of defending the deficits has not changed.

This is not to suggest that there should not be deficits from time to time. But they should be rare. They should be the exception to the rule and not the rule.

In 1796 Thomas Jefferson said that if he could add one amendment to the Constitution, it would be to restrict the borrowing power of the federal government. For most of the nation's history, there has been what sometimes is referred to as "the unwritten amendment," that we would balance the budget. From the beginning of the nation until 1917, we had accumulated a grand total of $3 billion worth of indebtedness. Sixty years later, we have now topped $2 trillion. In the last sixty years of our nation's history, we accumulated 666 times as much indebtedness as we did in the first 150 years of our history.

Thanks in large part to the leadership of Paul Volcker, chairman of the Federal Reserve Board, (and in part to huge imports, as well as oil price declines and unemployment) inflation is at least temporarily under control. But if we continue to escalate the federal indebtedness, foreign capital to purchase our debt eventually will be unavailable, and the pressure will be immense on the Federal Reserve Board to "solve" our problem by increasing the money supply excessively. That will bring about another round of inflation and major problems to the economy and, eventually, more unemployment. We can avoid that by avoiding the deficit growth that puts pressure on the Federal Reserve to simply print more money.

The permanent, annual interest expenditure caused by the increased deficit of just the last three fiscal years is approximately $50 billion a year. We will be spending $50 billion per year in perpetuity for our imprudence. That is seven times more than we spend on all our federal health research programs and three times more than we spend on all of our federal education programs. That $50 billion could guarantee a job opportunity to every American and still leave a huge balance for reducing the deficit, reducing the indebtedness, or providing a tax cut.

Fiscal policy includes tax policy, and in addition to striving for greater equity, tax policy should include the general goal of greater employment through four specific objectives:

1. *Greater stability.* Too frequent changing of the tax laws dis-

courages long-term planning and investment, and that results in loss of jobs and loss of international competitiveness.

2. *Encouragement of savings.* The savings rate of the nation hit an all-time low of 1.9 percent for one month in 1985, though we are generally around 6 percent. That compares with a savings rate of almost 13 percent in West Germany and 25 percent in Japan. Canada's savings rate is, roughly, double ours. Encouragement of savings will bring down the costs of capital. It takes substantial investment to create most jobs. Decrease the cost of that investment, and you make it easier for businesses to create more jobs. It is not automatic, but it is generally true. Jobs, productivity, and an ability to compete internationally are three horses that are tied together. We are much more likely to have those horses carry us into a brighter future if we become better savers.

3. *Emphasis on productivity and research, rather than merger.* The "mergermania" that has gripped the nation costs us greatly. Corporations that invest in new plants and research should be given tax breaks; those that simply gobble up other companies and add nothing to the nation's productive capacity do not deserve the tax breaks they are getting. The mergers almost always add to unemployment because with the merger comes some type of reorganization that lets people go.

Our policy on mergers should be geared to using capital wisely, to encouraging increased productivity and job creation. Those of us who are Democrats are particularly subject to criticism—legitimate criticism—that we have stressed more equitably dividing the economic pie rather than expanding it. If we do not add to the productive capacity of this nation, and only stress equity, the pieces will simply get smaller and smaller. We need a balance of both better distribution and improved productivity.

I also have concern about the common belief that we are becoming an "information society" rather than a society that produces things. There is some truth to this newly acquired wisdom, though our trade and tax and defense policies have aggravated the trend. In 1973, 26.2 percent of our employment was in manufacturing.

By 1986, it had dropped to 19.5 percent. That represents a drop
in the standard of living for most of the employees who have shifted
away from manufacturing—pay is almost always less—and it
represents a questionable policy for our nation. While I am pleased
to have good financial data, improved health care and other results
of a service-oriented society, I also recognize that I cannot eat
information, I cannot sit on service, I cannot drive in it either.
To maintain a quality standard of living, and to improve it, we
have to produce things that people consume. Our tax laws should
encourage that. That also creates jobs.

Our research efforts have slipped. Two decades ago the United
States spent roughly twice as large a percentage of our national
income on research and development as did Japan and West Germany. Today it is approximately the same as these two countries,
but that is a distorted figure. A sizable amount of our research
goes into the military where the economic rewards for the nation
are slim. West Germany and Japan devote dramatically less of
their research to the military and significantly more to research
on things that have a much greater market potential. The lead sentence in a *Washington Post* story about one university tells what
is happening in the nation: "Next spring, almost one-third of the
nation's best young engineers will leave the Massachusetts Institute
of Technology to begin designing weapons."[3] When defense is
excluded, Japan and West Germany are substantially ahead of us
in the percentage of their income spent on research. For the five
years beginning in 1980, U. S. civilian research increased 41 percent, defense research increased 95 percent. It is basic that in this
competitive world the nation that acquires new knowledge most
rapidly and applies it most rapidly moves ahead of the competition. The United States is slipping relative to our competition in
both acquisition and application of research. That eventually has
to mean loss of jobs.

We also need much greater cooperation on research between
government and the private sector. Read what former Secretary
of Commerce Philip Klutznick writes:[4]

The last time I looked at it we had over 600 governmental research facilities. . . . In Boulder, Colorado, is a very important laboratory concerned with atmospheric and other studies, including the laser beam. . .under the jurisdiction of the Department of Commerce. When I visited [it] during my tour of duty, the assistant director asked me a simple question: "I have been in the laboratory for 23 years and I would like to know, Mr. Secretary, why it is that we never see any of the leaders of industry come out here to see what we are trying to do?". . . . We have more unused science and technology than any nation in the world. . . . We must develop a concept that the government and production by private industry are not enemies but friends who cooperate with one another.

But that government-private industry cooperation must be led by industrial and government leaders who understand the importance of both production and research. Economist Hyman Minsky has commented, "Our leaders of industry are marketing and finance oriented. . .not production oriented."[5] Unfortunately, in too many industries that is the reality.

4. *Encouragement of labor-management cooperation.* Early in this century, at at time when steelworkers were working twelve hours a day, seven days a week, Judge Elbert Gary, head of U. S. Steel, commented with great inaccuracy that unions were obsolete. "They may have been justified in the long past, for. . .the workmen were not always treated justly," he said, but now he saw "no necessity for labor unions" and "no benefit or advantage through them will accrue to anyone except the union labor leaders."[6] Judge Gary was considered to be one of the more progressive industrial leaders of his day. He favored profit-sharing for his employees, a position ahead of most of today's industrial leaders. There has been tremendous improvement in conditions for laborers since his time (some of which Judge Gary helped to bring about), but we still have more labor-management friction

than is desirable, more than in most western industrialized democracies. We can encourage an improved relationship by sharing problems and profits.

The Employee Stock Option Plan—giving employees the chance for partial or full ownership of a company through purchase of its stock—as well as profit-sharing plans, should continue to be encouraged through our tax laws. Profit-sharing gives workers a stake in improving productivity and reduces friction. There is still substantial suspicion by both management and labor of profit-sharing. But its day must come. Labor-management committees, whatever their title, that work to improve the quality of life for employees and productivity for the company are almost always helpful. A survey by the Chamber of Commerce showed that 9 percent of the employees interviewed believed that if the productivity of the company they worked for improved, they would personally benefit. A similar study in Japan showed 93 percent of the Japanese workers were convinced they would benefit through improved productivity. We have a way to go! If we believe we can create many new jobs and remain competitive in the world today but pay no attention to productivity, we are deceiving ourselves. The surveys make clear that management, labor, the media, and government leaders have much to do in getting people to understand how our economy works and how we must move forward.

But whether it is tax policy to encourage better labor-management relations or encouragement of savings, the most basic fiscal policy change is still the obvious: generally, we should not spend more than we take in.

Trade Policy

The annual trade gap in 1985 reached an astounding $148 billion. The monthly figure for July, 1986, reached a record of $18 billion. If that figure were to prevail (and it will not) for the rest of 1986, the 1986 trade deficit would be an astronomical $198 billion. If you use the traditional measure of $30,000 in imports equals the loss of one job, that $148 billion 1985 trade gap caused the loss of 4,900,000 jobs. Even if you were to raise that figure to $40,000 a job, that still means the loss of 3,700,000 jobs. The present estimates are that the trade gap for 1986 will be $170 billion. Using the $30,000 per job measure that means the loss of 5,600,000 jobs; if you use the $40,000 measure, it means the loss of 4,250,000 jobs. There is some offset, however. If you buy a shirt made in Korea or Singapore rather than the United States for one dollar less, that one dollar can be used to buy other things, creating some additional jobs. But the job loss is still massive. By most conservative estimates, at least one-third of the unemployment in the United States today is caused by the trade gap.

Unfortunately, the economic ills caused by the trade gap are not quickly cured. When Caterpillar shifts some of its manufacturing to Brazil, Scotland and France in order to continue to compete in the international market primarily because of the overvalued dollar, once that dollar starts coming down, Caterpillar's overseas plants are not likely to be moved back to the United States. Third World customers who have found it economically advantageous to buy from Japan and France and Italy do not suddenly switch back to the United States when the dollar declines, particularly if they feel they are getting good service and good quality products from their new sources. Trade gaps leave economic wounds that take a long time to heal. The job loss is not quickly recovered.

The most important action we can take on the trade gap is to pay much more attention to it. More inattention will lead to continued drifting and continued high unemployment. Attention will lead to action. For years the United States did well in trade primarily by letting the private sector handle everything. The federal government sat on the sidelines like a benign father, occasionally paying some attention but not often. That day must quickly pass.

In specific terms, to close the trade gap we must take three actions:

1. *Reduce the federal fiscal deficit.* That deficit keeps interest rates up, relative to the rest of the world and causes the dollar

to be priced too high. The dollar is overvalued approximately 30 percent. That means a tax on everything going to other countries of 30 percent and a subsidy on everything coming in of 30 percent, at this writing. The overvalued dollar is probably responsible for half of the trade gap. The dollar is falling in value as this manuscript is being written, in large measure because the world financial market senses Congress and the Administration finally and belatedly are getting serious about putting our fiscal house in order. While there is a slight inflationary impact with the falling dollar, at this point the trade deficit is a much more serious threat to the U. S. and to the world economy than is inflation. A falling dollar will not immediately close the trade gap and bring back jobs. There will be a substantial time lag as the world's businesses first wait to see whether the drop in the dollar's value is more than momentary, and then when they feel some security in the new value, there is a gap between the time of new orders and job creation. Damage to the economy and the loss of jobs were not created overnight, and they will not be reconstructed overnight.

2. *Come out of our cultural isolation.* We are the only nation on the face of the earth in which you can go to grade school, high school, and college and eventually get a Ph.D., and never have a year of a foreign language. That must change. You can buy in any language, but to sell you have to speak the language of your customer. It is a simple lesson too many American businesses have not learned. And those businesses reflect our cultural provincialism. Recently, I visited with a successful American business leader who showed me his catalog of products with great pride. In nineteen years he had built a small retail store into a major American manufacturing enterprise. I asked how much of his business was exports. "Only about two or three percent," he replied. "We take orders from others in English if they come to us, but we have not solicited it." He is representative of too many American businesses. Trade has not been a high priority of most segments of the U. S. business community. Our policy of economic and cultural isolation, where we accept the business of others only if they come

to us, must change. We must also recognize that increasingly technological breakthroughs will come from other countries. If U. S. business is to stay on top of things, we must carefully monitor the technical journals of other countries, attend their seminars, and move away from an attitude of comfortable superiority. Our interest in other languages and cultures should start in the early grade school years, something that is part of the curriculum in almost all other nations. Fewer than one percent of U. S. grade school pupils study foreign languages. In most countries, all elementary school students take foreign languages.*

3. *Get tougher in trade negotiations.* In trade policy we are still living in the immediate post-World War II era when we made generous trade concessions to the rest of the world, almost all of which was desperately poor. I still favor trade concessions to poor nations: Bangladesh, Mauritania, and many others. But they are not the source of our trade difficulties. As nations move into the status of being relatively well off, we should insist on either free trade or parity. An American car sent to Japan takes three months for inspection approval; a Japanese car sent to the United States requires thirty minutes. When the President announced that we would become the only nation with a significant automobile market not to have a quota on Japanese cars, I called a friend in the White House to ask what we got in return. He replied, "Good will." If Japan had reduced her absurdly high tariff and quota barriers on beef or pork or other products, I would have understood. We can no longer trade something real for something as amorphous as good will. I like good will, but we can retain that by sensible, hard bargaining not by senseless generosity. The Japanese have a trade strategy; we have none. We simply react. Canada charges us a 30 percent tariff on catalogs printed in the United States; we charge Canada nothing. Canada charges us fifty cents a hundredweight for nails; we charge Canada five cents a hundredweight.

---

*For more information about this problem, see the author's book, *The Tongue-Tied American*, (New York: Continuum, 1980).

I favor free trade. But if we cannot get that, we must protect American workers. If Canada charges us five cents for nails, we must charge them five cents; if they charge us fifty cents, we should charge them the same. In fact, the threat of that possibility is likely to produce reduced barriers on their part.

A danger of not having a more sensible trade policy is that the pendulum can swing from its present extreme to the opposite extreme of protectionism. Everyone will be a loser if that happens. That need for a middle ground is stressed by former Trade Representative Robert Strauss, and he is right.

One of this century's great senators, Paul H. Douglas, also was a leading economist and former president of the American Economic Association. He drafted a letter sent to President Herbert Hoover, opposing the high-tariff Smoot-Hawley Tariff bill. The letter was signed by most of the nation's leading economists. Douglas favored free trade, but he also authored a provision in a major trade bill, the Trade Expansion Act of 1962, that gave the President authority to raise tariffs as well as reduce them. President Kennedy did not favor having this authority to raise tariffs, but Douglas felt it was essential to have the ability to threaten tariff increases in order to force other countries to stop practices that erected trade barriers in a one-sided way. He felt it was the only practical way to bring nations with unfair trade practices to the negotiating table. Without using that weapon or threatening to use it, Douglas reasoned, the trade picture would get out of balance. How right he was.

State Department decision-making on trade and tariff policy is dictated solely by the desire to build good relations, rather than economic reality. In theory, the State Department is not in charge of trade, but in fact, it is. This has to change. We must listen to the Secretary of Commerce. Our trade representative should not be a distant, peripheral figure in an administration. At the May, 1986, Tokyo summit meeting, President Reagan and other world leaders issued a fine-sounding statement on encouraging sounder trade policies but, unfortunately, no one even bothered to invite the U. S. trade representative to be present for the discussions. Responsibility for trade policy is now scattered among at least eighteen governmental entities in which trade is a second-rate priority. It is difficult to differ with the conclusion of President Reagan's Commission on Industrial Competitiveness: "Fragmented trade policy responsibility in the United States seriously limits our ability to respond to the growing volume and complexity of international trade."[7] Senator Ernest F. Hollings of South Carolina has suggested that we create a National Trade Council to coordinate efforts, just as we have a National Security Council to coordinate security activities. It is a practical way of accomplishing a needed objective without getting into the turf wars that can paralyze any attempts at change.

Education

Economist Lester Thurow summed up our situation well: "A second-class poorly educated American labor force is not going to beat first-class well-educated German, French, or Japanese labor forces. America invented high-quality mass public education; America is going to have to reinvent it."[8]

The United States cannot remain a first-rate economic power with significant growth in our standard of living without paying greater attention to our number one resource, the human resource. In general, people who are more highly educated are more productive and earn more money. If we want to lift the productive capacity of the nation and compete with the rest of the world, we must lift the educational level. There is a saying about computers: "Garbage in, garbage out." Modify it a little, and it can apply to our economy: Poor quality in, poor quality out. One of the wisest persons I know, Milton Katz, a retired Harvard professor, says that what is best about high school athletics is that it is the only part of the high school agenda where quality is really stressed. If you don't measure up, you don't make the team. There is a germ of truth there. Standards of excellence and high performance too often are not demanded of students or teachers or parents.

A Nation at Risk is the accurate title of a 1983 report to President Reagan, describing our educational situation. Where are we today?

— Of the 158 countries in the United Nations, we are 49th in our literacy rate. An officer of the First National Bank of Boston recently commented that two-thirds of those applying for jobs at his bank cannot fill out the application form.

— Attending elementary and secondary school in Japan requires 240 days a year, compared to an average of 180 days a year in the United States. In the Soviet Union, you attend elementary and secondary school six days a week; in the United States, it is five. Do we really believe that we can stay ahead of others with less emphasis on education?

— In the United States, three-fourths of high school seniors spend less than five hours a week on homework. In Japan, almost three-fourths of the high school seniors spend substantially more time on homework.

— Graduates of secondary school in the Soviet Union have four years of physics. In the United States, 16 percent of those who graduate from high school have one year of physics. In the United States there are more school districts than there are physics teachers.

— A 1981-82 fourteen-nation test of mathematics skills at the eighth grade level found U. S. students third from the bottom. Algebra and calculus tests for twelfth graders in the same countries showed the United States last.

— A 1985 report from the Committee on Economic Development, comments: "Employers in both large and small businesses decry the lack of preparation for work among the nation's high school graduates. Too many students lack reading, writing, and mathematical skills, positive attitudes toward work, and appropriate behavior on the job. Nor have they learned how to learn, how to solve problems, make decisions, or set priorities. Many high school graduates are virtually unemployable, even at today's minimum wage."[9]

— Richard J. Mahoney, Chief Executive Officer of Monsanto, wants schools to "start tackling how to help the students who fail to complete high school...over one million unequipped entrants to the workforce each year.... While many schools feel it is their duty to teach students how to drive a car, few feel it is their obligation to teach students how to get and keep a job."[10]

— We spend a smaller percent of our national income retraining workers than any Western industrialized democracy.

— In the United States, seven of every one thousand college graduates receive degrees in engineering. In Japan, it is forty of every one thousand. Japan, with half our population, graduates twice as many electrical engineers as does the United States.

— In Chicago's public schools, of those who start high school, 47 percent of the Hispanics, 45 percent of the blacks, 34 percent of the whites, and 19 percent of the Asian-Americans do not complete high school. Nationally, 29 percent of those who start high school do not finish. Fewer than 5 percent of those in Japan who start high school do not finish. The unemployment rate for U. S. dropouts is roughly 60 percent for the first few years after leaving school. What that means in terms of crime in the communities, no one knows, but the costs are staggering. Approximately 85 percent of those in Illinois prisons have not graduated from high school. The figures in other states are similar.

— One editorial observer has accurately noted: "In survey after survey, poor schools and poor public safety outrank high taxes and congestion as the prime reasons for business flight [from the cities]."[11] The writer might also have noted that there is a direct relationship between poor schools and poor public safety.

— In most developed countries, the pay differential between a teacher and an engineer or a physician or an architect or a lawyer is not nearly as large as in the United States. We say through our pay scale—and in other ways—that we do not prize teachers highly. One of the finest teachers I know says that teachers generally feel they are undervalued by society, and it is difficult to come to any other conclusion. Not surprisingly, the result is that many of the finest teachers leave the profession. We are attracting too few of the really bright, able young people into the field. The long-run significance of this for the nation is awesome.

Perhaps most troubling of all, the public schools reflect the public. When we show indifference to the quality of education, the results should not surprise anyone. A public not concerned about foreign languages and science and math is going to get schools where those subjects are not high priorities. A public more concerned with who the third baseman is for the St. Louis Cardinals than who the third grade teacher is for their children is going to end up with highly paid, quality third basemen and underpaid, sometimes less-than-quality third grade teachers. The quality of third basemen says almost nothing about the future of the nation; the quality of third grade teachers says everything about the future of the nation.

Positive things have happened, however. Our education system has opened opportunity to many. Perhaps the most striking illustration is that earned income of black males was 43 percent of white males in 1940, and by 1980, it had risen to 73 percent, the greatest gains coming from those who had seized educational opportunities. Seventy-three percent is still not as high as it should be—and female income and family income have not shown such dramatic gains— but, nevertheless, the educational system has opened opportunities and made possible substantial gains. In a few inner-city, low-income elementary schools, there are some startling success stories, as measured by the traditional test scores. The two major teachers organizations, the National Education Association and the American Federation of Teachers, are not only responding favorably to new ideas but are helping to initiate ideas. The days of rigid adherence to the status quo appears to be becoming an unhappy part of history, not the path for the future.

Also encouraging is that many of the parents in the most economically deprived sections of our cities are willing to make substantial sacrifices to get their children into schools that are demanding in terms of curriculum and discipline. Some of these central city schools are excellent. Recently I spoke to a student body gathering of Jefferson Junior High School in Washington, D.C. There were approximately eight hundred students in attendance, from a virtually all-black school. Students obviously had their orders for silence, and it was completely quiet—a not too common occurrence at school assemblies anywhere. Questions from the students were exceptionally good. A superficial visit and judgment, yes. But I came away with a solid impression about the educational opportunity these young people are being given.

A note from my brother about one of his sons who attends an urban public school tells part of the good side of today's education: "Richard's second grade experience was so good that on the last day the entire class broke down and wept because it was all over and so did the teacher. So did Richard when he went to bed that night, and one other parent in the class told me the same of her child."[12]

While there are good things happening in education, any candid analyst has to come to the conclusion that in the United States, we have not made education a high enough priority. We are going to have to invest more of our time and more of our resources in education and do both more wisely.

Here is what we should focus on to solve this problem.

Attack illiteracy vigorously.

A conservative estimate is that 23 million Americans can read a stop sign but cannot address an envelope, cannot fill out an employment form, and, perhaps worst of all, cannot help their children with school work. This perpetuates the generation-to-generation pattern of too many citizens poorly prepared to help themselves or our economy. There is mounting evidence that we are adding approximately a million more to the illiteracy lists each year. Of those who can read and write, large numbers of adults cannot read and write above the fifth grade level. Illinois has 5 percent of the nation's population, and in our state the estimate is that two million adults are at the fifth grade literacy level or below. Multiply that figure times the national population, and the sum is an astounding forty million.

A St. Louis employment official describes the typical chronically unemployed person he deals with as "a school dropout before the ninth grade, who is on a third-grade reading and academic level."[13] To the surprise of no one, it is hard to get a job for that person.

An observer of the Chicago prison scene commented, "I think that not being literate is the cause of a lot of people being here. If you can't read or write or correctly fill out a job application, one thing leads to another."[14]

A few weeks after the overthrow of the dictator of Haiti, "Baby Doc" Duvalier, the Roman Catholic bishops of that country announced a program to eliminate illiteracy in Haiti in the next five years. Haiti is two-thirds illiterate. We don't know what the results will be, but if impoverished Haiti can face her problem and act upon it, why can't the rich, sleeping giant called the United States awaken to our problem and do something?

Former Secretary of State Henry Kissinger headed a group of distinguished Americans looking at the problems of Central America. The Kissinger Commission made a series of recommendations, but the only recommendation to make the news was one to provide a greater weapons supply to the Contras in Nicaragua, a recommendation that surprised no one since the Administration had carefully appointed the commission. But almost unnoticed was a recommendation to establish a literacy corps to help the nations of Central America. I applaud that suggestion— but why not also have a literacy corps for the United States?

Here's a fairly typical story. It's not dramatic, but it tells of one man and of what could happen in the nation. Most people in Quincy, Illinois, probably believe that everyone in their community can read. If there's a problem, it's "somewhere else." The *Quincy Herald-Whig* reports:[15]

Clifton Anders, a bagger at the Kroger store in Quincy has a dream.

He wants to learn how to operate a cash register so he can work as a "checker" in one of the supermarket's check-out lanes. As a checker, he can earn a lot more money than he can as a bagger.

But Anders knows he must be able to read before he can get such a job.

At 29, he's trying his best.

For the past eight months, Anders has been working with a volunteer tutor so he can finally—after all these years—learn how to read.

Anders, the father of two, is making great headway in his efforts to read. Not long ago, he learned enough about reading to pass his driver's license test for the first time. And he sees even more doors opening up in the future.

"Maybe some day soon I'll be ready to put my feet behind the register," Anders smiled Friday as he shared his dream. . . .

"I'm so happy I got into the literacy program," he said. "I felt real shut out when I went places and had to read."

What a change in the life of Clifton Anders! Multiply that times millions, and you understand what a change that could mean in the cultural and economic life of the nation. And you can be sure those two Anders children are being taught to read—a long-term payoff for them and for the nation.

Steven Pickett dropped out of school in the ninth grade because he couldn't read and was getting nothing out of school. He managed to get several jobs and finally ended up as a crane operator for U. S. Steel. But when U. S. Steel offered him a promotion to fore-man, he had to turn it down because being a foreman would require filling out forms. He never took a trip anywhere because he couldn't read the signs. When he discovered his son having reading problems in school, thirty-three-year-old Steven Pickett decided to learn to read and went to the City Colleges of Chicago for help. Fortunately, that help was available. But Steve Pickett's story is the exception, not the rule.

A few of us have been able to achieve some small legislative steps forward on literacy at the federal level, and state and local efforts and voluntary organizations are doing good work. It is probably an optimistic estimate to guess that all of these efforts combined are reaching 2 percent of the people in need. A few corporations like B. Dalton Bookseller and Time, Inc., and Gulf and Western have provided leadership. Pat Robertson's religious group is working on this. These efforts—laudable as they are— are almost like the proverbial "spitting in the ocean." To have a sustained, deep impact, there must be more than scattered, voluntary efforts. *Government must recognize illiteracy as the major plague it is.* The director of personnel at General Motors estimates that 30 percent of its workforce is either illiterate or close to it. He adds, "Business pays three times for poor public education. Once in tax dollars—a second time in lost productivity and creativity on the job—and a third time when we have to fill the educational gaps ourselves with in-house education and training programs."[16]

Illiteracy is a hidden problem. The people who can't read and write are ashamed of that fact and go out of their way to hide it. You learn that they cannot read and write when you ask them to sign a paper, or they stare at a newspaper you hand them pretending to read but obviously trying to hide the truth. Note this story from the *New York Times:* "A herd of beef cattle was destroyed by accident in Chicago. A feedlot worker could not read the labels on the bags that he found piled in the warehouse and fed poison to the cattle by mistake. He thought that he was adding a nutrition supplement to their feed basins."[17]

A massive national effort to eliminate illiteracy within five years is both needed and achievable. The results would be startling for the economy and to the families of these people.

Experiments are in order. For example, for one year in two states we could have every person who signed up for welfare or unemployment compensation or food stamps fill out a form, and if he or she cannot read and write, a special effort should be made to enroll anyone in that family who needs help in basic education programs. In two states we might try an experiment, making a special one-time bonus payment of $200 to those on welfare who pass their high school equivalency tests. For families on welfare for more than one year in two states, we might offer a bonus of $250 for each child in that family who passes a basic literacy test. Governor Baliles of Virginia has inaugurated a plan to insist that no one gets a parole from prison until he or she can pass a basic literacy program, a powerful incentive to study in an atmosphere where social pressures now are against studying. A host of creative things can be done, but we are basically not addressing the problem.

The unemployment rate for those who cannot read and write is dramatically higher than for those who can, though I know of no one who has compiled the full statistics, a strange phenomenon in itself. We know exactly how many cattle have hoof-and-mouth disease, but we don't have any idea how many unemployed human beings cannot read and write. We do know that the majority of people in our prisons are functionally illiterate. We know that the average earnings for those who cannot read and write are substantially lower than for those who can.

The nation is paying a price in crime, a price in lost productivity, a price in despair for our failure to launch a major effort on this problem.[18]

Prize teachers more highly.

Try this: Ask the ten brightest high school students you know what they want to become. You will hear a variety of answers, but it is unlikely any will respond that they want to become teachers. That is part of the national picture. Underpaid and undervalued, the profession is slipping in its appeal to bright students. College entrance tests show this dramatically. Studies in North Carolina and Wisconsin show that too often those leaving the profession are the best and brightest teachers. The average teacher is in the field less than seven years.

An article surveying the Far East notes that "in Japan, where competition for teaching positions is rigorous, only university students with good academic records can apply, while in the U. S. teachers are usually drawn from the less academically able, as measured by scholastic aptitude tests. Japanese teachers are relatively well paid in comparison with other professions."[19] In Japan, teachers are paid more than the average college graduate receives; in the United States, appreciably less. In Japan, teachers are in the top 10 percent of citizens in income; in the United States, teachers are only slightly above the national average.

Compounding the U. S. problem is the reality that we soon will have a serious shortage of teachers. At a time when we should be raising pay and raising standards, the temptation will be to "solve" the problem by lowering standards. The difference in starting pay for a teacher-graduate and a lawyer-graduate or engineer-graduate becomes even more startling in later years. It is not unusual for an outstanding lawyer to make $150,00 a year. It is unusual for an outstanding teacher to make $35,000 a year.

Teaching is perhaps the only profession in which you can be outstanding and get rewarded by leaving the profession—to become a principal. When I speak to a group of school administrators, I often ask the question, "How many of you would rather be teaching if you could receive the same salary?" Usually half the hands go up. Similarly, we have excellent first grade teachers who go into high school teaching because the financial rewards, and public respect, are greater there. We need outstanding instructors at the elementary level fully as much as we need them in our high schools.

If we want the best for our children, we cannot get it by inadequate pay and little thanks. Thanking a teacher is one of the simple things we can do. When teachers describe their job as "thankless," that is sometimes literally true. (It should be noted that despite all of the problems, this nation continues to have a host of dedicated and able teachers.) Improving the lot of teachers will come primarily from state and local governments, not the federal government. But together we must provide answers. Education must become a priority.

One small suggestion: In each elementary school and high school, the school board could set aside $2,000 to $3,000 to pick the "teacher of the year" selected by fellow faculty members. The money would go to a teacher for summer travel to other countries. A different teacher should be selected each year with the understanding that each year a teacher would visit a different area and that the awardee would teach for at least two more years. The life of that school will be enriched, and teachers would receive a tangible and psychological award for distinguished service.

It is difficult to exaggerate the value of a good teacher. Those who work hard, set high expectations for their students, show enthusiasm, and somehow inspire their students, make a contribution beyond calculation. We should mine our society for such teachers and treasure them highly.

Help problem learners earlier.

The evidence is overwhelming that helping students when they are in academic difficulty as freshmen in high school is fine, and there should be such help available, but the problems ought to be spotted much earlier. As soon as low achievement is noted, special help should be provided. Generally, that should be long before high school. In Chicago, for example, three out of every four freshmen in high school read below the national average. At Orr High School it is 96 percent, and at sixteen other high schools in Chicago it is over 90 percent. A *Chicago Tribune* article on the school system notes, "The greatest obstacle to education, however, is that many students have little incentive to learn. They see no future reward in the form of a good job, or any job at all."[20]

Middle-class whites pay too little attention to the schools, either because their children have already graduated or because they are attending private schools. There is little realization that their indifference is building a grim future for the city—and the nation. Mayor Tom Bradley of Los Angeles has even suggested the possibility of establishing public boarding schools to break the cycle. A public school system geared to stable families, and children eager to learn, is not coping effectively with children who don't fit that pattern. Chicago is not alone. The most promising answer found so far is the preschool program.

In John Naisbitt's book *Megatrends,* he says that you can look at Florida and see what the nation will be like in 1995. In that state two-thirds of the recipients of Aid to Families with Dependent Children (AFDC) are not high school graduates. If we seriously want to reduce AFDC costs, we should help people with difficulties—or potential difficulties—with their school work, and do it before they formally enter school.

Preschool programs to assist children in low-performance neighborhoods ultimately will have tremendous rewards. There is no disputing that reality. There is also no disputing the fact that we are doing little to follow through on this knowledge.

Federal programs to promote preschool education should be substantially enlarged.

A *Chicago Tribune* editorial put it well:[21]

A strong national commitment to early childhood education is the surest way to break the chain of chronic poverty. And it would pay off in several major ways. It would markedly increase the ability of disadvantaged children to succeed in school and lessen their need for expensive special education. It would raise the odds that these youngsters would avoid the traps of academic failure, delinquency, teenage pregnancy, drug abuse, unemployment and chronic dependence on welfare. . . .

In the mid-1960s, researchers in Ypsilanti began to study 123 young children considered to be at high risk of failing once they started school. All came from poor black families. They scored low on IQ tests. Few of their parents had finished high school. Half of the families were on welfare. Almost half were headed by single parents.

Half of these youngsters were enrolled in high-quality preschool programs five mornings a week, either for one year when they were 4 years old or for two years at ages 3 and 4. A visiting teacher also spent 90 minutes a week in each child's home helping a parent provide more learning opportunities. The other youngsters got no preschool education.

Ever since, researchers have followed the progress of both groups. The first reports confirmed that those with the early learning opportunities got better grades and fewer failing marks. They were absent less from school. They needed less special education. And they had a better attitude toward school than a group of similar youngsters who did not get the preschooling.

A second payoff has just been documented, now that the groups have reached age 19. The long-range data show that those who had the preschool education were much more likely than the others to have finished high school and to score average or above on competency tests. More of them had jobs or were involved in higher education. And they were less likely to have been arrested, to be on welfare or to be pregnant.

Because they needed less remedial and special education, it actually cost less to educate the children who got the preschooling than those who didn't, even when the expense of the early classes was included. Researchers report preschool cut the cost per student of each succeeding year in school by about 20 percent—about $800 per child every year in savings.

In terms of reduced crime alone, taxpayers will save $3,100 for every one of the young people who got the preschool training, researchers estimate. These are the direct costs of the criminal justice system and don't count the anguish, fear and physical suffering that criminals can inflict on victims. Nor does it attempt to measure the psychological benefits of a reduction in crime rate in a community or any subsequent cutback in private security systems.

Taxpayers have already saved seven times the cost of one

year of preschool education in the Ypsilanti project and three and one-half times the tab for two years. And the savings resulting from reduced needs for welfare, from less crime and from greater ability to earn will continue for the rest of the lives of these young people—and even reach into the lives of the following generation.

The dollar costs to the nation of school failure, remedial education, delinquency, crime, premarital pregnancy and welfare dependency are staggering. The human costs are even greater. The evidence is clear that early childhood education can prevent at least some of these problems from ever occurring—and save considerable money doing so. The time has come to act on this compelling evidence.

A New York University study of 178 young people, nineteen to twenty-one years of age, some of whom had participated in extensive Head Start programs and some of whom had not, shows a striking parallel to the Michigan study. The payoff is overwhelming—in the opportunities for these people and in a healthier society and economy for our country.

Three centuries ago, Comenius wrote: "If we want to educate a person in virtue we must polish him at a tender age. And if someone is to advance toward wisdom he must be opened up for it in the first years of his life."[22]

Brookline, Massachusetts, School Superintendent Charles Slater said, "The issue is no longer whether we will serve younger children. The only question is how we will do it."[23]

Missouri now requires local school districts to employ child development specialists who visit and work with parents from as early as three weeks after birth. Missouri is the first state to do this, but inevitably others will follow, for the evidence is overwhelming that waiting too long is costly in both economic and human terms.

If we are serious about wanting to avoid having unemployed adults, greater attention will have to be paid to young people before the age of eight. A national effort to identify people who need help in their early years and then provide it, would pay off more slowly than some programs. The long-term pay-off is clear. National leadership as well as state and community and volunteer efforts are needed. If this requires one-on-one efforts in the case of some children to make sure they can learn to read, let's do it. The American public is ready for such leadership.

Expand adult education programs.

The need for training and retraining and further retraining will grow. Richard J. Mahoney, chief executive officer of Monsanto, has expressed concern for "America's ability to redeploy workers who are affected by changing technologies and markets. These changes have shifted the dynamics of many industries. One of my tasks as the head of a large company is to make sure our strategies and resources are adjusted to meet changing conditions. As a nation we must do the same."[24]

Studies show that a majority of high school dropouts would like to obtain further schooling, but they find it awkward. We should assist them with that option. Community colleges are particularly helpful in reaching the adult population, though many are not reaching out as much as they should be. Businesses could be of help in this process by urging employees to continue their schooling, whether they have finished only the fifth grade or have done some college work. Businesses can encourage this through working out flexible hours, bringing instructors onto the industrial location, offering to subsidize tuition or a part of it, or providing transportation. Several major corporations in the Minneapolis area do this, as well as others throughout the nation. More businesses should follow their example. A particularly outstanding example of business leadership is the Boston Compact. Under this agreement the businesses of the Boston area have pledged to provide a job to every student in Boston who graduates from high school, a powerful, practical incentive for students to stay and graduate.

Not only does encouraging education among their employees enrich the nation, but businesses find that they end up with more satisifed employees and pay out less money in unemployment compensation. Employees who leave a job are statistically more likely to find a job quickly as the educational level rises. Even a small ceremony or note in the company paper about people who have passed their high school equivalency test or have completed some special course unrelated to the business is helpful.

John McCloud, a nineteen-year-old high school dropout, had been told by a judge that as part of his probation he had to go back to school at least part-time. His tests showed third grade reading level and fourth grade math level. His self-esteem was even lower. He had been placed in special education programs in school. He went to the Tri-County Urban League Learning Center in Peoria, Illinois, on orders of the judge. There they discovered that one of his problems was poor eyesight. Glasses provided under the federal government's Job Training Partnership Act (JTPA) and just ninety-nine hours of instruction brought him from a third grade reading level to the sixth grade, from a fourth grade math level to the seventh grade. He now has a forty-hour-a-week job at four dollars per hour and is extremely happy. He is going to night school at the nearest high school. The John McClouds are out there, and when we reach them, everyone benefits.

The JTPA program helped John McCloud, and it has been effective in helping others, but it has two liabilities. First, JTPA is reaching only a small percentage of the people it should be reaching. Second, while the payoff from this program that primarily trains people out of work for available jobs is good, as more marginal workers are trained for jobs that are less certain, the short-run payoff will not be as dramatic, though the long-term benefits are clear. The program's critics will grow in number as JTPA reaches out more.

The predecessor to JTPA was the Comprehensive Employment and Training Act (CETA) that needed improvement but received more criticism than it deserved. CETA reached many people the JTPA program is not reaching. As programs—such as CETA— reach out more and more to the people who really need help, there are unfortunately fewer and fewer defenders of the programs. The anecdotal stories of abuse—as in food stamps and other programs for poor people—diminish their political popularity. Now JTPA is being attacked because it "primarily transfers the cost of job training from the private sector to the public sector," not a fair charge and not likely to be the main criticism as JTPA does a better job and reaches the people who need help the most.[25]

Expand work/education programs and strengthen vocational education.

Cooperative education programs in which high school youth go to school and work part time, usually getting credit for their work, have been remarkably successful. This takes extra work for school administrators and for the businesses, but by any measure it pays off: fewer dropouts, the chance for students to learn about working, the opportunity for businesses to get good help inexpensively and evaluate possible future employees. These programs work well at the college level also. Northeastern University of Massachusetts conducts the largest program and an amazingly successful one.

Vocational education programs need to be strengthened, expanded, and more creative approaches should be tried. We have a well-structured system for those who go on to college after high school. We essentially have no system for those who are not college-bound. Vocational programs should include an adequate academic base. Businesses want employees who are more than one-dimensional, and the training base should be broad enough so that a new skill can be acquired if the demand for the recently acquired skill disappears, and that will frequently happen. Finding the proper balance is not easy. Too much academic work, and the student may leave school; too little, and the student's future is severely limited. Usually, if you can get a student really interested in one course, he or she is unlikely to become a drop-out. Vocational education has its critics, and sometimes those critics are right. Sometimes reading and writing and arithmetic skills are not stressed; sometimes good work habits are not communicated; and sometimes vocational education programs are designed for yesterday's needs rather than today's or tomorrow's. Vocational education, like anything else, can get in a rut and not change with the needs and the times. But a well-planned, practical, vocational education program—in tune with the world of work—can offer good background and employment opportunity.

Encourage stability and enrichment.

In *A Nation of Strangers,* author Vance Packard suggested that a major reason for the high crime rates in the United States is our propensity for constantly moving. We do not live anywhere long enough to have real roots, to have a sense of embarrassment or shame if someone in the family violates community norms. We tend to view having a very mobile society as a great national asset. In some ways it is. But it is also a national liability. It is not uncommon in a few inner-city schools to have more than a 100 percent turnover in students in one year, and a turnover of more than 50 percent is common. How can a teacher really get to know the students or the parents? One experimental suggestion has been made: Pay parents in inner-city school districts one hundred dollars at the end of the year if a student has been in that school all year and has a good attendance and tardiness record. One education writer comments, "We pay farmers not to farm. Why not pay parents not to move?"[26] While that statement is not completely fair to farmers, a two-year trial of such a program in one or two urban areas could prove beneficial. It is the type of experimenting in education that almost never takes place. If education were on the New York Stock Exchange, few people would buy the stock because such a small percentage of the expenditure is on research.

One major American city, with a long waiting list for public housing, is considering an experiment. Families in which students have good school attendance records will get preference for housing. Will it work? I don't know, but that type of experimentation should take place much more.

Along with stability should come enrichment programs that are more than the basic and routine. In rural school districts it is common for the local PTA or the band parents or some other organization to help provide the added little things that can improve a school. It is uncommon in urban schools. Parents do not feel as much a part of the school and sometimes of the community. Getting parents and administrators and teachers and neighborhood leaders together to work on a trip to Washington, D.C., or an astronomy program or an adult reading program or some special cultural enrichment features helps the school in two ways: It provides the immediate enrichment program, and it improves and increases communication between school officials and parents and community leaders. In some cases that communication is almost nonexistent. At Orr High School on the West Side of Chicago there are two thousand students. The school has a PTA with twenty members. Graduating classes each year number only approximately two hundred.

Every college has an endowment or foundation program. We never think about such possibilities for public schools. Carefully structured to prevent abuse, it could attract funding that would provide long-term enrichment for schools that desperately need such enrichment.

Stress quality and access in higher education.

For the next eight years the nation's changing population pattern will cause a significant drop in the numbers of those in the 18-22 age bracket. That drop in college-age students probably will result in lowering of standards by some colleges eager to acquire students to bolster sagging enrollments. Lowering standards is obviously a dangerous course for the struggling college and for the nation. But it is not the only problem we face in higher education. Others include:

— College tuition is rising more rapidly than assistance to students. The result is a declining percentage of minority students and white students from lower-income families attending college, a major long-range loss for the nation. Even students from middle-income families are sometimes dropping out because everyone does not fit into the comfortable categories student grant and loan programs spell out. A student may come from a family where the parents have an income of $40,000 a year, but the parents are separated, though not legally separated, and the chief wage-earner is unwilling to help the son or daughter. The complex scenarios of real life are endless, and young people are too often missing an opportunity to develop themselves. In addition, this financial squeeze is causing higher education in our nation to become increasingly segregated on the basis of economics, those from upper-income families attending non-public colleges and universities, those from lower income families attending the public institutions. This is not a healthy trend for the nation.

— Too many students are studying law. In 1970, we had 270,000 lawyers in the nation, in 1985 we had 640,000. Thirty-nine thousand are graduating from law school each year. Too much stress on law saps other areas of bright minds and tends to involve us in far too much litigation. Those studying law will increasingly be forced into other fields. The United States has thirty times as many lawyers for every 10,000 people as does Japan.

— Graduate schools' costs discourage many fine students from continuing their education. In 1960, 23 percent of graduate engineering students awarded doctorates in our country were foreign students. Today it is 55 percent. In 1965, 14 percent of graduate chemistry students awarded doctorates were foreign students. Today it is 39 percent. There are similar statistics in physics and mathematics.

— In many engineering schools in the United States, the majority of graduate students are from other nations. Some stay here. The majority return to their home country. We welcome foreign students, but when fewer and fewer U. S. students are preparing themselves for their own and our nation's long-range future, that is a signal of problems ahead. One way to change this picture is to extend to graduate school the student assistance programs now available only to undergraduate students.

— The share of research dollars in our universities devoted to basic research is declining. The director of the National Science Foundation has accurately assessed this situation: "Failure to provide substantial support for basic research and education is sure to have grave consequences."[27]

For those interested in learning more about where we are and what should be done for elementary and secondary education, there have been a number of excellent reports. The one I would recommend most highly is *Investing In Our Children* published in 1985 by the Committee for Economic Development, 477 Madison Avenue, New York, New York 10022. Written for the business community, but helpful to any serious observer, it is practical and realistic about where we are and what needs to be done.

The United States cannot provide more jobs and more meaningful jobs for our people, cannot improve our productivity and our competitiveness with the rest of the world, unless quality education becomes a much higher priority. There are few things in policy-making where you can say with absolute certainty that you are right. This is one of them.

Tying It Together

Improvement in fiscal policy, trade policy, and education policy will help put our citizens back to work and help to lay a better foundation for the fundamental program that is needed, the Guaranteed Job Opportunity Program. In addition to these three major policy areas, other changes that could help lay that foundation and improve the nation's employment picture include:

— Dealing with the sensitive illegal immigration problem. Jobs secured by undocumented aliens often are those that unskilled U. S. citizens could fill. One recent study suggested that for every 100 workers illegally present and employed in the United States, sixty-five American workers are displaced. In Chicago, for example, it is estimated that there are approximately 135,000 citizens of other countries in the United States illegally holding jobs. If the 65 percent replacement factor of the recent study is reduced to 60 percent, that still means 81,000 jobs that are lost. Immigration laws have to be worked out carefully—and the programs must include greater cooperation to lift the economy of Mexico in particular—but a significant source of unemployment is the worker who is not here legally.

— Improving the U. S. Employment Service. In some places it does a superb job. In others not so good. Less than 20 percent of job openings come to them, only 5 percent of the jobs listed nationally are through them. A stronger, more imaginative operation is needed. (Forty percent of jobs are found through word-of-mouth.)

— Creative blending of job needs and job seekers. A Chicago neighborhood organization visited eighty apartments in an area of great poverty and high unemployment. Mostly women were interviewed, and many had worked in a hospital or nursing home or some aspect of home health care. The neighborhood organization put an advertisement in a nearby middle-class neighborhood newspaper which read, "Health Care Workers Available," and the response was dramatic. Within a week all of those with health care skills were employed—and all within eight blocks of their homes.[28]

— Encouragement for the creation, development and growth of small businesses. Most small businesses that "fail" do not cause any loss to their creditors. Only one out of eight businesses that "fails" ends up owing money. While they are in business all eight employ people and add to the income and production of the nation. And those businesses that "succeed" do even more. Those who look at business "failures" only in negative terms should recognize the positive contribution that even the less successful enterprises make to the nation. Small businesses give the nation most of its new jobs and new products. The growth in the number of small businesses has been good, but it could be better. Great Britain and France have programs to encourage the unemployed to start their own small businesses. It has worked. The French success rate for unemployed people going into a small business is over 60 percent, and the British success rate is almost 90 percent, though those high success rates are possible only because of careful screening.

— Providing advance notice before plants are closed or before there are sizable numbers of layoffs, helping employees, and permitting faster retraining and job placement, and reducing unemployment insurance costs for employers and taxpayers.

— Providing some type of voluntary set-aside for further training and education, whether it is an Individual Training Account, as some advocate, or whether it is simply a negotiated set-aside such as the United Auto Workers has with Ford or the National Union of Hospital and Health Care Workers has in New York City. Herbert S. Donow, president of the Western Egyptian Central Labor Council of Illinois, has suggested a program called "Moving Up" to encourage workers to upgrade themselves and make use of their potential more fully. Most education and training programs focus on the young and disadvantaged. But part of lifting both opportunity and productivity should be focusing attention also on those who are doing moderately well but could be doing better. Some greater financial assistance for training, further education, or even going into a small business would help everyone.

— Finding and encouraging really top-quality personnel, a need for both education and industry. Much of this book discusses lifting the disadvantaged. But encouraging those with the potential to be really outstanding, who can make important contributions to a better society, also needs more attention.

— Planning much more, in both the public sector and the private sector. Not stultifying, rigid central planning but sensible, flexible long-range planning. Healthier communities and more jobs will result.

The list of additions to fiscal, trade, and education policies that have an impact on employment could be a long one. Whatever list is put together will be helpful, but not adequate by itself. One major piece of the puzzle is missing: the Guaranteed Job Opportunity Program discussed in the next chapter.

Endnotes

1. Ronald Reagan, address to the nation, Jan. 25, 1986, text from Associated Press wire.

2. *Jobs for the Hard-to-Employ, A Statement on National Policy* (New York: Committee for Economic Development, 1978), p. 12.

3. Fred Hiatt and Rick Atkinson, "Arms and America's Fortunes," *Washington Post,* Dec. 1, 1985.

4. Philip Klutznick, letter to Paul Simon, Jan. 10, 1986.

5. Prof. Hyman Minsky, Washington University, St. Louis. Note on manuscript to Paul Simon, July 14, 1986.

6. David Brody, *Steelworkers in America: The Nonunion Era* (Cambridge, MA: Harvard, 1960), p. 175.

7. *Report of the President's Commission on Industrial Competitiveness* (Washington: Government Printing Office, 1985), Vol. 1, p. 39.

8. Lester Thurow, *The Zero-Sum Solution* (New York: Simon and Schuster, 1985), p. 88.

9. Report of the Committee for Economic Development, *Investing In Our Children* (New York, 1985), p. 2.

10. Richard J. Mahoney, letter to Paul Simon, Feb. 11, 1986.

11. "Key to Crime, Schools," editorial, *Chicago Tribune,* Dec. 24, 1984.

12. Arthur Simon, letter to Paul Simon, undated but sent August, 1986.

13. Mickey Rosen, quoted by Gregory B. Freeman, "Chronically Unemployed Lack Basic Education," *St. Louis Post-Dispatch,* Dec. 23, 1985.

14. Louis Gross, quoted by Sandra Crockett, "If More Inmates Could Read," *Chicago Defender,* Dec. 1, 1985.

15. Edward Husar, "Adults Who Can't Read Speak Against Illiteracy," *Qunicy Herald-Whig,* Sept. 14, 1985.

16. William C. Brooks, General Director of Personnel Administration at General Motors and Chairman of 70001, in the keynote speech to the Hudson Institute Center for Education and Employment Policy's conference, "Prepar-

ing Youth for the Job Market of the Future,'' Oct. 3, 1985, Indianapolis, Indiana.

17. *New York Times,* Aug. 19, 1982, quoted by Jonathan Kozol, *Illiterate America* (New York: Anchor Press/Doubleday, 1985), p. 13.

18. Readers interested in learning more about this problem are urged to read Jonathan Kozol's book *Illiterate America.*

19. Gene Gregory, ''Japan's Education Edge,'' excerpted from the *Far Eastern Economic Review* of Hong Kong in *World Press Review,* Feb. 1984.

20. Patrick Reardon and Jean Davidson, ''Schools Promote Few From Poverty,'' *Chicago Tribune,* Sept. 30, 1985.

21. ''Preschooling Payoffs,'' editorial, *Chicago Tribune,* Dec. 29, 1984.

22. Comenius, *The Great Didactic,* quoted in *What Works* (Washington: U. S. Department of Education, 1986), p. 6.

23. Quoted in ''Early Schooling Is Now the Rage, by Edward B. Fiske, ''Education Life'' supplement, *New York Times,* Apr. 13, 1986.

24. Richard J. Mahoney, letter to Paul Simon, Feb. 11, 1986.

25. ''Son of CETA,'' by James Bovard, *The New Republic,* Apr. 14, 1986.

26. Aaron Cohodes, ''Let's Pay Parents to Keep Their Kids in One School,'' *Nation's Schools,* August 1969.

27. Statement of Erich Bloch to the Senate Committee on Labor and Human Resources, Mar. 26, 1986.

28. ''Why Can't the Poor Be Productive?'' by William Raspberry, *Miami Herald,* Jan. 8, 1986, quoting from a report by John McNight in *Chicago* magazine.

Chapter Four

The Essential Element: A Guaranteed Job Opportunity Program

We need a national effort against chronic poverty that goes beyond dollars and fear. There has always been a strong sense in this country, among conservatives as well as liberals, that every American deserves a chance to build a decent life. Conservatives, in particular, know that it should not come in the form of a handout, but as an opportunity a person can seize and develop.
—Chicago Tribune editorial[1]

Full employment is the foundation of a just economy. . . . We must make it possible as a nation for everyone who is seeking a job to find employment. . . . Employment is a basic right, a right which protects the freedom of all to participate in the economic life of society.
—National Conference of Catholic Bishops, June 4, 1986[2]

Clearly, there is a need for a comprehensive national employment policy.
—American Association for Counseling and Development, January 24, 1986[3]

THREE REALITIES should cause a change in our national employment policy: First, the demand for unskilled labor is declining. That trend will not change. Second, the pool of unskilled labor is growing. We can eventually change this reality with better education and training and retraining programs. Because changing it will be slow, we should work to change it much more aggressively. Third, we are not going to let people starve.

Faced with those three realities, we have a choice of paying people for doing nothing or paying people for doing something. It makes infinitely more sense to pay people for doing something, to let them be productive, to let them know and feel that they are needed and contributing toward a better society.

Separately, we know the truth of those three statements. But we never seem to put them together. We must. In 1985, Senator Daniel Evans of Washington and Governor Charles Robb of Virginia chaired the Committee on Federalism and National Purpose that recommended: "Launch a major effort to make employment programs more effective in helping welfare recipients to become self-supporting through work. To the maximum extent possible, convert welfare systems into job systems."[4]

Giving people—not just those on welfare—a chance to work is so obviously sensible, yet we move reluctantly in that direction. The day must pass when political leaders can simply ignore the massive problems of the least fortunate in our society. The irony is that when polled, the public believes in providing a job guarantee to all Americans. Their instincts are sound. They do not know how complicated it is—and it is complicated. They do not know how much it will cost, but they instinctively understand that not doing it will cost a great deal more. It will increase the productive capacity of the nation immensely. The public agrees with Professor Gary Orfield of the University of Chicago: "Public-service employment is better than having people on welfare."[5]

What we do *not* need is a program that provides temporary relief but adds to the national deficit, creating greater problems in the long run. We *do* need programs that add to the productivity of the country, that make our nation more competitive in the world market. A solid, sensible, fiscally prudent, productive program can be put together and should be put together.

To the extent possible—and much more is possible—we should be encouraging jobs in the private sector. I am a former businessman. I believe in the free enterprise system. Most of the suggestions that were made in chapter 3 are designed to encourage the private sector to provide more jobs. Encouraging employment in the private sector as the better alternative has been written about by a host of authors. I applaud their efforts at stimulating us to do a better job. But where private sector jobs are not available, the answer of our society should be something better than, "Sit at home, and we'll send you a check."

The day we begin guaranteeing a job opportunity to every American will not bring about the millenium, any more than the eight-hour day and child labor laws did, but like those changes, guaranteeing a job opportunity will be a giant step forward for this country, the next giant step forward. Properly drafted and executed, it will reduce crime, eliminate some of the most severe poverty, help millions of Americans lift their standard of living, enrich the nation through the productivity of those now unproductive, and generally help the economy of this nation.

The cynics will cry, "It won't work." It has been their lamentation from the beginning of time. The cynics are not going to build a better world. You and I can.

A nation creative enough to get the blessing and curse of television into virtually every home, to bring electricity into those same homes, to substantially raise the standard of living of almost all of our citizens in half a century—such a nation can also guarantee a job opportunity to all of its citizens if it simply makes it a matter of national priority.

But it has not been a priority.

How do we get there?

We need to move on several fronts at once, the three outlined in the previous chapter—trade, fiscal policy, and education—among them. A Guaranteed Job Opportunity Program created in isolation could work, but it would be expensive and not do as much good as a coordinated assault on our basic ills. Unemployment is the visible evidence of those ills. If we deal only with the results of our problems but ignore the causes, we will have helped the nation but not as much as we can and should.

Assuming that an integrated assault on our problems is launched, an essential part of that assault should be a jobs program.

What I propose is a Guaranteed Job Opportunity Program that will make a job available to any citizen eighteen years of age or older who qualifies, paying the minimum wage for thirty-two hours a week, or 10 percent above welfare payments or unemployment compensation, whichever is highest. It would lift many out of poverty, increase the standard of living of all who participate, make productive citizens out of those now involuntarily non-productive, and permit millions to sense accurately that they are contributing to a better society rather than detracting from it.

Jobs in the private sector should be stimulated, but when those jobs do not develop, the Guaranteed Job Opportunity Program can put people to work productively, teaching others how to read and write, helping with day care centers, planting trees, assisting in senior citizens programs, cleaning grafitti off the walls of subways, cleaning off vacant lots, making bicycle trails, and doing a host of other things that will improve our society.

We have these needs, and we have unemployed people who want to work. Why not put them together!

The Outline of the Plan

Authorized and financed by the federal government, the Guaranteed Job Opportunity Program would work like this:

— The governor of each state appoints a committee of seven to hold hearings on what the appropriate governing districts within the state should be. They could be the same geographical districts the Private Industrial Council district of the JTPA (Job Training Partnership Act) now has, or they could be different geographical districts.

— In each district an executive council of thirteen people will be appointed. Four are appointed by the governor, two from each political party; four are appointed by the mayor of the largest city within the geographical district, two from each political party; and five are appointed jointly by the chief executives of the other governmental units within the district, no more than three from any one political party. At least four of the thirteen must represent the business community, and at least four must represent labor unions.

— The thirteen-person council is authorized to employ an administrator and necessary support personnel, but in no event will the administrative and personnel costs exceed 10 percent of the money paid for putting unemployed people to work. The personnel employed in a professional capacity within the district will be subject to the restraint-from-politics restrictions now applicable to federal civil service employees. At least one person in administration will be a counselor. Careful auditing will be required.

— Jobs will be provided on a project-by-project basis, following guidelines on the projects established by the Secretary of Labor. Within those guidelines, the local council can select projects. Any project may be vetoed if two labor union council members file an objection with the district council, or if two business members of the council file an objection.

— Supervisors will be employed on a project-by-project basis and will be paid the local prevailing wage.

— To be eligible to work within a district a person must have resided there at least thirty days and must have been out of work at least thirty-five days immediately prior to employment under this plan.

— No more than two people in any one household are eligible for a job. No one in a household with more than $17,000 annual current income is eligible.

— Those eligible unemployed who are hired will work a maximum of thirty-two hours per week under this program. They will be paid the minimum wage (currently $3.35 per hour, $107.20 per week), or 10 percent above what they receive under welfare if they are on welfare (if that is higher than the minimum wage), or 10 percent above what they would receive under unemployment compensation if they are eligible for unemployment compensation (if that is higher). When they become ineligible either for welfare or unemployment compensation, they will continue eligiblity for the thirty-two hour program at the minimum wage until they are once again employed full time.

— The council may reduce the thirty-two hour requirement for the $107.20 per week stipend in unusual cases if the work assigned is generally paid more in an area for a skill the unemployed person has.

— Only those who are high school graduates or non-graduates eighteen years of age or older will be eligible. Those between eighteen and twenty-five who are not high school graduates will be required to take tests to determine their verbal and mathematical skill levels. They will receive counseling and be required to attend evening or weekend clases until they receive their high school equivalency diploma.

— All applicants of whatever age will be tested for basic reading and writing ability. Those who cannot read or write or have limited skills will be encouraged to improve themselves. Brief but basic training in applying for a job, how to prepare a resume, and the practical steps to take to search for a job will be provided all applicants. ''Job Clubs'' may be formed in some areas where people get together with one another to discuss what they are doing, encouraging one another. There have been some extemely successful experiments along this line.

— Transportation and equipment for a project cannot exceed 10 percent of the cost of a project. Anything above that amount in equipment needs or construction material must be provided by the state or local government.

— An unemployed person given a job under this program may work up to sixteen hours per week in another job or jobs.

— No one will be eligible for the Guaranteed Job Opportunity Program without having shown evidence of trying to secure employment in the private sector. No one can stay under the program without providing evidence of that continued pursuit.

— Those eligible must be citizens of the United States or aliens legally authorized to work.

— Those employed under the Guaranteed Job Opportunity Program will receive medical coverage (the ''green card,'' if they meet standard eligibility requirements) unless they have coverage through private, part-time employment, other government programs, or through other members of their family.

— Whether many people on welfare will be required to sign up for the Guaranteed Job Opportunity Program when it is fully implemented will be up to the states. States will find that the voluntary movement off welfare will be significant. Eventually, most states will probably require that all but mothers with children under two or three must sign up for the Guaranteed Job Opportunity Program. Oklahoma now requires "Workfare" for mothers within weeks of the birth of a child.

— Food stamp regulations would remain unchanged. Some people working under this program would be eligible, some would become ineligible because of increased income. The same would be true for energy assistance.

— Supervisors may give job references—the first job reference some of these under the program will ever have had—and a more recent job reference for others who don't want to give a reference for a job held years ago.

— Unemployed people given jobs will receive Social Security coverage to maintain eligiblity for both the retirement and disability programs but will not be covered by unemployment compensation.

— People eligible for retirement payments under Social Security, Railroad Retirement or any other retirement program will not be eligible to participate in the program, unless that retirement program pays less than $400 a month. Those old enough to receive Social Security but not eligible for retirement payments can work long enough to fill out the necessary quarters of work to become eligible.

The program will be administered by the Department of Labor. No new federal agency needs to be created.

How Would It Work in Practice?

Let's take Johnson County, Illinois, population 9,960. Its county seat is Vienna, population 1,420. Its unemployment rate in 1985 averaged 14.4 percent, varying widely from 11.4 percent one month to 19.4 percent. Of 3,725 listed as workers in the county, 525 are now unemployed. An additional 100 people probably are "discouraged workers," unemployed but not counted. Perhaps fifty work part-time so infrequently that they are virtually unemployed. The county is almost all white. It has 401 people on AFDC and ninety-five drawing general assistance, with small numbers in other income-assistance welfare programs.

Assuming that the national averages prevail in Johnson County (which may not be the case), 29 percent (152) of those jobless are receiving unemployment compensation, and 42 percent (220) have been unemployed less than thirty-five days.

Johnson County probably will be joined with two or three or four other small counties to form the administrative district for carrying out the Guaranteed Job Opportunity Program. The people of Johnson County will be solicited for their ideas for projects for their county. These will then be sifted and refined by the council. In Johnson County the program might emerge in this way:

Total officially unemployed	525
"Discouraged workers" (people out of work but who have given up)	100
Grand Total Unemployed	625
Those unemployed less than five weeks, not eligible for the program	220
One-half of those who are drawing unemployment compensation who would prefer that to the job opportunity program alternative	76
Total not using the program	296
Potential net jobs needed in Johnson Co.	329

Johnson County has twice the national average for unemployment so the picture is more grim and more difficult than for the population as a whole. But even in a hard-hit area like this, it means creating 329 jobs in a county of 10,000 people, not an impossible task. What kind of jobs could be created?

Infrastructure jobs (outlined later in this chapter)	70
Construction of a bicycle path in the Shawnee National Forest	50
Tutor the illiterate	30
Tutor adults with limited skills to improve those skills	20
Tutor grade school and high school students who need special help	20
Assist in schools by helping teach another language and culture (for foreign language-speaking citizens)	5
Assist in day care centers for children so unemployed single parents can seek and accept employment	20
Assist in day care centers for seniors to allow people with dependent parents to work	20
Assist in program and path clearance at Ferne Clyffe State Park	10
Assist in clearing ditches along rural roads	10
Assist in recreational development of Dutchman Lake	15
Repair sidewalks	30
Tear down condemned buildings	30
Clean up old, neglected cemeteries	5
Insulate homes for older citizens and those in need; work with the public utility to pay for materials through utility savings	25
Clean up trash along the county highways	20

    Plant seedlings for citizens who want more
        trees or plant them on public lands   10
    Develop arts programs   5

That totals 395 jobs, more than the 329 people that, in theory, might seek jobs under the program in Johnson County. Since all those who might need the jobs will not want them, the actual figure will be significantly less than 395. A creative group of a dozen Johnson County citizens could get together and come up with plans that could put twice that number of people to work. In any community with major unemployment, there are also significant opportunities to improve the community.

Most of these jobs are of limited duration. When the cemeteries are cleaned up, and people are still unemployed, then the local committee will find another project. There will be no shortage of opportunities for projects. A project-orientation for jobs gives people a chance to feel that they are contributing something concrete, which they are; it avoids the assignment of people to a governmental unit, an easy "solution" that too easily leads to purposeless work and substitution for paid workers; and by moving from project to project, people learn to develop different interests and job skills, in addition to good work habits.

Some suggest that the answer for these people in Johnson County is to move where there are jobs. We have had a great deal of that, and it has caused the massive concentration of poverty in the cities that is bad for the cities and bad for the nation. The Guaranteed Job Opportunity Program probably will reduce mobility in the nation a little, but that is good! If there really is a good job waiting in Houston or Denver, people will move from Johnson County. But there is less likelihood they will move in desperation and simply on the basis of hope.

But, you argue, Johnson County, Illinois, is not Chicago or Pittsburgh or even Boise.

True, but the urban arena offers advantages for jobs projects that Johnson County does not. No governing district for the program should get so large that it is beyond effective control. Cities should be broken down into smaller areas. But the urban area provides easier transportation from one district to another than Johnson County. Special opportunities or needs in a neighboring district are only a bus ride or a subway stop away. In Chicago or Pittsburgh the program could assemble an orchestra to play at schools or in the neighborhoods, or convert abandoned rail beds into bikeways. That would be difficult to accomplish under this program in Johnson County. In cities, project employees could clean graffiti from the walls of subways and simply by their presence add to security in subways. In cities there are more people who speak other languages than there are in rural areas. You could take ten or twenty Polish-speaking unemployed people with some academic background, and have them visit largely black elementary schools, spending four weeks at each school, giving these young people an exposure to another culture and another language. There is a much greater need in urban areas for literacy assistance, for people to clean up parks, for day care help, for simple programs that can be worked out with the police to reduce crime. Cleaning vacant lots and destroying abandoned residences are needs in most cities. Anti-rodent efforts would help. Urban areas have more people who can teach sculpture and other art forms. We tend to define work too restrictively. Work is anything that improves the quality of life. If Israel had not included music as work, Itzhak Perlman, who had polio, would not be enriching the world with his violin playing today. No, the barrier to moving ahead is not whether the area is urban or rural or a mixture. The barrier is our unresponsiveness and our lack of creativity.

Most people—contrary to the public myth—receive less under welfare than they would at the minimum wage for thirty-two hours. Many can also find private sector, part-time work to assist in their finances under the Guaranteed Job Opportunity Program. Illinois—more generous than most states—pays $385 a month for a family of four on AFDC. The average family on AFDC in Illinois receives $304.96 a month. Under the Guaranteed Job Opportunity Program, one person in that family would earn $464.53 a month at the minimum wage, plus whatever part-time work he or she could get.

The reason for establishing thirty-two hours rather than forty hours—four days a week rather than five—is to have one traditional working day free to pursue other job opportunities. Even if another job is a private-sector minimum wage job at forty hours, that is a 25 percent increase in income over the government job. The stress should be on finding private-sector employment if possible, but if it is not possible, there is this alternative.

How Does This Differ from Workfare?

Workfare is the label generally given to programs that require those receiving welfare to do public service work.

A Guaranteed Job Opportunity Program differs from Workfare in several respects.

Workfare applies only to people on welfare and keeps them at whatever the welfare pay is. Workfare is an improvement only in the sense of getting someone into good work habits, an important assist, but Workfare does not offer much hope for anything better coming along.

The Guaranteed Job Opportunity Program differs from Workfare in many ways:

— It offers a national wage rate, or 10 percent above welfare or unemployment compensation, whichever is greater. It gives people an incentive to work by paying them more than they would receive under welfare or unemployment compensation.

— A person does not have to be on welfare to be eligible.

— Counseling is available to help a person improve his or her economic lot.

— Careful educational testing is required so that those needing assistance to improve verbal or arithmetic skills can receive that, or someone in need of a high school equivalency or other training program can receive that. Those over twenty-five would receive more limited tests but would be encouraged to improve themselves educationally.

— Special services sometimes will be offered under the Guaranteed Job Opportunity Program, such as day-care and transportation. Workfare ordinarily does not offer such assistance.

— Workfare has the image of being punitive and mean-spirited, not offering a real lift to those who work. The Guaranteed Job Opportunity Program offers both a financial advantage and educational counseling help.

But, you ask, under the Guaranteed Job Opportunity Program, what about people who do not have good work habits, who do not show up on time for a job, who show they cannot be assigned a job?

First, if they do not show up, or do not work when they do show up, as in any other job, they will lose it. Because the program often will be dealing with people who are not accustomed to the rigors of work, losing a job may not be uncommon, and counseling often will have to take place. Working with those without job habits sometimes will not be easy. Those in charge must be firm. One-on-one assistance and leadership occasionally will be required.

For some there should also be an alternative, a day-to-day work opportunity with greater supervision. People can be referred to this when they fail in an earlier job assignment. Once that person shows greater reliability, he or she can be referred to another more regular Guaranteed Job Opportunity Program position. As a boy in Oregon, I went to the unemployment office each morning in the summer to see what jobs were available that day. This day-to-day alternative work opportunity would be something similar. But the incentive and the rewards would go to those who work well, as they should.

How Will This Program Affect the Unemployed?

George and Emma Loomis are both unemployed and have three children. They are on welfare. They receive $424 a month to cover all of their expenses. Assuming they can work something out for their children—the oldest is eleven—and both work under the Guaranteed Job Opportunity Program, between them they would receive

$928.06 a month. If between the two of them they can also pick up part-time odd jobs to bring in at least twenty dollars a week, that makes their total earnings just over one thousand dollars a month—not great but a significant improvement. More important, it gets both parents into the work attitude and discussing other job possibilities where they can make more money. It brings a new pride to the family. For George and Emma Loomis, this is a chance to get out of a rut of despair.

George and Emma Loomis and other single or married parents will find child care facilities developing in their communities under this program. Some of the people who work in the centers can be under the Guaranteed Job Opportunity Program. State and local governments, school districts, local religious groups and others will receive encouragement to assist in this important task, not simply with custodial care but with enrichment programs for the children. It should be added, however, that in many communities there is a tendency to exaggerate the demand for day care facilities. Many people like George and Emma Loomis decide to leave their children with grandparents or other relatives and friends rather than at the child care facility, no matter how fine it is.

Tom Dobers is twenty-seven, single, drawing $80.28 a week unemployment compensation and having a real struggle. This program permits him to increase his income to $107.20 a week, and since it is a thirty-two hour week, he can spend that fifth work day going around to explore better work possibilities. Tom's former employer also would benefit. Tom's taking the public sector option means less liability on the employer's future unemployment compensation payments, because the experience factor that sets the employer's rate will be improved.

Sarah Symms looks older than her thirty-one years. She has five children. She yearns for affection and sees no hope for herself. She has never been married though she lived with one man for four years. She receives $523 a month in welfare payments for herself and her five children. She dropped out of high school and sees no purpose in going back. "I wasn't much good anyway," she comments. If she works part-time, most of it is taken off her welfare check the next month. So she does not work at all. She has just given up, and she appears to be transferring that despair to her five children. Sometimes she talks about moving away from her rural community to Chicago, but it is not with the hope of getting a job. She has no such hopes. The Guaranteed Job Opportunity Program would increase her income by 10 percent over her welfare check, to a total of $641.30. She would be encouraged to get her high school equivalency certificate. Counselors would not only work with her but work with school and day care personnel to see what could be done to enrich and upgrade the lives of her children. Any extra money she earns from part-time work she could keep. As she improves her skills and gets more confidence in herself, she would transfer some of that new confidence to her children and, inevitably, she would look for a better job. In the meantime, she starts to accumulate some credits for her Social Security retirement, a distant thing for a thirty-one-year-old, but for the first time she has earned money and has something more positive toward which to look. This job opportunity is not great for her, but it is better.

John Snyder is fifty-eight and lost his job as a coal miner when the mine shut down. He made more than $25,000 a year when he worked, which was not regularly. His wife is not in good health but gets help from the United Mine Workers health program. John is waiting for word that a new coal mine will open, though the chances are slim they will hire a fifty-eight-year-old. He and his wife have three grown children, all married, all having a real struggle with family finances. They're not in a situation to help John and his wife, and John would be embarrassed to ask even if they were. The life savings that he and his wife had, ''to take a trip over to the old country'' when he retired, is gradually being used up just for survival. He has a savings account with $1,100, owns a four-year-old car and has two years of mortage payments yet on their modest home. Fortunately, the mortgage payments are only $184 a month. But it is $184 they don't have. They have too much to be eligible for welfare, and John says, "I'll die first before I go on welfare." That $107.20 per week that John Snyder could get under the Guaranteed Job Opportunity Program would tide him over until he becomes eligible for his miner's pension and Social Security.

Laura Smith is slightly retarded. She is twenty-six and lives in a unit of a public housing authority designed by a man of unusual compassion and vision, designed specifically to permit fairly independent living for people like Laura. A pleasant person, Laura can carry on a conversation and can do limited work assignments. Her parents are still living and support her. But one of these days, Laura is probably destined to fall on the welfare rolls because our society has not had the good sense to make use of Laura's limited abilities. Instead of paying her for doing nothing, the Guaranteed Job Opportunity Program could find a task for her that would match her skills. She should be a productive member of society. Giving her something useful to do is good for the taxpayers and is good for Laura's self-esteem. There are some whose mental or phsyical disabilities are so great that they cannot perform as Laura can, or be helped by a sheltered workshop. But there are hundreds of thousands of Lauras who yearn to contribute, to be proud of themselves, who are now a drain on society. Needlessly.

Thirty-one-year-old Patricia Cartwright is afflicted with arthritis, badly enough that it is visible. She lives on the fifth floor of a tenement house on the Lower East Side of Manhattan. When she goes up to her apartment—coming down is easier—she has to pause after each flight. One day as she paused, she was robbed by two teenagers. She blames it on them and her arthritis. She shares her apartment with another woman, and the only apartment they can afford is on the top floor of their building. So she faces those stairs every day. She has been on welfare almost seventeen months, long enough that when she applies for a job, employers "don't want to hire anyone who has been out of work for a year and a half." And they see her arthritis. They ask her about it. They never give that as the reason for not hiring her, but she believes that it often is. Between the seventeen-month job wait, the arthritis, and the stairs, Patricia Cartwright has almost given up hope. The Guaranteed Job Opportunity Program would increase her income slightly and give her a new lease on life. "If I had a four-day-a-week job, I'd be in heaven," she exclaims. Well, not quite. But it would give her a step up economically instead of another shove down. And having made one step up the ladder, she probably would be looking for the next step up.

Lisa Matthews is fifty-four. Her husband died six years ago. She has two grown children and a son who has just started college. Until he turned sixteen, she received Social Security benefits. Now she does not know where to turn. She has not worked since before her marriage. Her husband, a professional man, received an above-average income but, unfortunately, was not prudent with his investments and his income. She is obviously embarrassed to tell you her story. She is a woman with a great deal of pride. A job opportunity program could help her get started. She could go on welfare, but that really does not make sense for her or for society.

There are so many others, people who do not fit the comfortable categories we imagine. There is George who is a hard worker, his former employers will tell you, but who has a short temper and does not get along easily with fellow employees or his bosses. He gets fired. He knows he shouldn't lose his temper but he does. We have "solved" the problem by putting him and his family on welfare—not good for anyone.

Leon is not mentally retarded but close to it. His wife is about the same. They have six children. He does odd jobs occasionally for farmers in the area. They say he is a hard worker, but you never know whether he will show up. Leon sometimes shows up at homes in the neighborhood and says that they don't have anything to feed their children. Leon and his family are on welfare.

George and Leon are not likely to ever be outstanding workers, but they could be contributing at least a little to society under the Guaranteed Job Opportunity Program. It would give them the chance for pride, and Leon could learn better work habits and maybe get a permanent job with one of those farmers. And through counseling, maybe George could learn to control his temper problems. George and Leon are never going to be brought out as shining examples of what a program did for people, but everyone does not fit into those neat little categories about which journalists like to editorialize.

The average family on AFDC in the nation receives $340.23 a month, as of April, 1985. The $464.53 a month under the Guaranteed Job Opportunity Program would be higher than in all states except Alaska, California, Minnesota, and Wisconsin. When you add the encouragement to part-time work and the 10 percent above the welfare payment or unemployment compensation provision, there literally should be no family that would not be better off under this proposal. The average AFDC monthly payment per family as of April, 1985, on a state-by-state basis is:[6]

Alabama	$113.37
Alaska	597.68
Arizona	213.78
Arkansas	153.18
California	506.83
Colorado	300.80
Connecticut	462.79
Delaware	242.55
District of Columbia	295.99
Florida	227.16
Georgia	190.93
Hawaii	403.04
Idaho	263.28
Illinois	304.96
Indiana	224.83
Iowa	336.14
Kansas	298.94
Kentucky	194.26
Louisiana	169.59
Maine	339.25
Maryland	275.85

Massachusetts 372.22
Michigan 455.86
Minnesota 476.14
Mississippi 92.76
Missouri 251.73
Montana 309.65
Nebraska 319.99
Nevada 195.29
New Hampshire 310.39
New Jersey 347.40
New Mexico 233.33
New York 451.36
North Carolina 199.06
North Dakota 345.10
Ohio 291.22
Oklahoma 260.90
Oregon 324.72
Pennsylvania 336.26
Rhode Island 424.95
South Carolina 183.00
South Dakota 255.42
Tennessee 131.00
Texas 158.57
Utah 320.34
Vermont 405.27
Virginia 236.40
Washington 424.32
West Virginia 196.29
Wisconsin 480.51
Wyoming 307.49

But Aren't These Dead-End Jobs?

They are and they are not.

They are not in the sense that there is encouragement to move from these jobs to private-sector jobs that pay more. They are not in the sense that testing and educational incentives and counseling will be offered with these jobs so that a person's potential can be more fulfilled.

But it should be added that millions of Americans work in what many people consider "dead-end" jobs. Sometimes they like the jobs and sometimes they don't like the jobs. Digging ditches may be viewed as a dead-end job to many people. But it is a useful and needed function in our society. And there are hundreds of thousands of Americans right now who would welcome an opportunity to earn money by digging ditches.

These dead-end jobs also pay money that permits mortgage payments to be made and keeps food on the table for a family and buys shoes for the children—and increasingly pays for college tuition for the young people in the family.

The easy categorization of some needed functions in our society as dead-end jobs is usually done by white-collar people whose contributions sometimes are less beneficial to society than those who perform these dead-end jobs. Someone has to sweep the floors; someone has to clean the toilets; someone has to dig ditches.

For the comfortably employed to put down a jobs program for the unemployed by references to dead-end jobs show both a lack of sensitivity and a fundamental lack of understanding of how our society functions.

If by dead-end jobs the critics mean positions where people stand around and do nothing, that is not a valid criticism of the Guaranteed Job Opportunity Program. That criticism had some validity for CETA, where people were simply assigned to a unit of government, whether there was something meaningful to do or not. Sometimes CETA workers had nothing to do and were paid for doing nothing—precisely what we do under present welfare policies. But with a project-oriented Guaranteed Job Opportunity Program, people are not assigned indefinitely to a unit of government but are assigned to a project. When the project is completed, then there is a new assignment.

The Guaranteed Job Opportunity Program gives people an opportunity to contribute in a meaningful way, and learn good work habits. Let the critics come up with a better answer!

How Would the Program Affect Family Life?

The present welfare policies discourage ''normal'' family life. A man with a $13,000 a year job may stay away from the mother of his children and his children because if he lives with them, she loses her welfare check. To what extent the pattern of living apart is a cultural phenomenon, rather than a way to get around welfare regulations, is not clear. What is clear is that children in one-parent homes are generally at a significant disadvantage. One study came to these devastating conclusions: ''One-parent children, on the whole, show lower achievement in school than their two-parent peers. . . . Among all two-parent children, 30 percent were ranked as high achievers, compared to only 17 percent of one-parent children. . . . Only 24 percent of two-parent children were low achievers—while fully 40 percent of the one-parent children fell in that category. . . One-parent children. . .are more than twice as likely as two-parent children to give up on school altogether.''[7]

Whatever the cause of the growth of one-parent households, its effects are clear.

I wish I could promise that the Guaranteed Job Opportunity Program would significantly change that picture. I cannot. I can say that there is more encouragement for a family to stay together. In the illustration I used a few paragraphs ago, the man with the $13,000 a year job could stay with his family, and his wife would be eligible for employment. If his income were $18,000, she would not be eligible.

Under a Guaranteed Job Opportunity Program, there could be a dramatic expansion of day care programs, permitting two people in a family to earn money, improving opportunities for women particularly to earn money. Financial problems are a major cause of family break-ups, and the Guaranteed Job Opportunity Program eases that cause of tension.

The lower your income, the less likely you are to live in the traditional family situation. To the extent that the Guaranteed Job Opportunity Program lifts income (and gives more meaning to life), it lifts the probability of families staying together. Combine that reality with the 1953-64 study showing a surprising relationship between unemployment and family separation (referred to on page 17 of chapter 1), and there is reason to hope for improvement.

We can gauge precisely what will happen to a family's income through a Guaranteed Job Opportunity Program. We also know that when we reduce poverty and unemployment, we increase family stability. Measuring that family impact in advance is not possible.

But this program provides a positive nudge.

Building and Rebuilding Our Basics

Accompanying a Guaranteed Job Opportunity Program should be a plan to work on the infrastructure—the mass transit systems and highways and bridges and sewers and water systems—of our country. By meeting these real needs, we also put people back to work.

There are also less obvious needs.

Within my lifetime (I am fifty-seven), I have seen rural America change from a land that was largely dark at night, with no electric refrigeration and other conveniences, to an attractive area where life is not appreciably different for those in rural homes than for those in the cities and suburbs. That did not happen accidentally. Someone had to have a dream.

Clean drinking water is now almost as universally available as electricity. Someone had to dream of having clean drinking water.

Dreams We Can Bring About

We should include telephones in our dreams of the future. Many people in cities and rural areas cannot afford a telephone. When

someone tries to force his way into a home or apartment for burglary or worse, there is no phone to use to call for help. When
someone in the household suffers a heart seizure, there is no phone
to provide instant communication to a doctor or ambulance. When
a fire is discovered, there is no way to call the fire department.
When someone is lonely and despondent and contemplating suicide,
that possibly fatal loneliness cannot be penetrated with a phone.
For almost seven million American homes a telephone is still an
unaffordable luxury. If, as seems likely, basic phone service costs
escalate in the near future as a result of the break-up of AT&T,
the number of homes without telephone service will rise.

Telephones can now be set so that you can use them only for
local calls, not long-distance calls. If you were to put a two percent surcharge on our long-distance calls and use the money to
provide phones that do not have long-distance ability to the less
fortunate among us, we could reduce crime, provide safety for
a health or fire emergency, enrich the lives of many of our citizens—and provide jobs to tens of thousands of people. Today only
about 40 percent of the phones sold in the United States are built
in the United States. While in general I am a free trader, when
the federal government is the purchaser, we should ordinarily
demand a U. S.-built product, and that would increase jobs in the
nation.

A six-cent increase in the gasoline tax would provide $7 billion
in revenue. One-third could go for rural roads and bridges, one-
third for state highway systems, and one-third for our mass transit systems. That would include all costs and put more than 200,000
people to work. More than half a century ago, a great U. S.
Senator, George Norris of Nebraska, said, "I would rather have
the government build highways and give men jobs than to take
the same amount of money and give it as charity to people who
are without jobs."[8]

In thousands of communities water systems need to be repaired
and extended, and sewer systems that were designed to take much
smaller loads are decaying, in addition to being inadequate. A

similar growth in expenditure—$7 billion—can produce a similar number of jobs, 200,000. It could be paid through dedicating part of the natural growth of the federal revenue toward this goal. Or a small tax on a commodity (such as liquor or tobacco) could produce it.

Congressman John Seiberling of Ohio pioneered an effort to establish an American Conservation Corps, a program designed to help the nation's parks and forests and to give young people a chance to contribute at a modest wage, similar to the Civilian Conservation Corps (CCC) of the 1930s. For less than $200 million a year, 85,000 young people could be given that opportunity. The entire nation would benefit. Educational enrichment should be part of this. The proposal at one point passed both the House and Senate. Teenagers are only 7 percent of the work force, but their unemployment rate exceeds all other groups except for the disabled. The unemployment rate for black teenagers is 40 percent and for Hispanic teenagers is 24 percent.

Initiate these four programs alone, and more than half a million Americans now out of work can go back to being productive and paying taxes instead of receiving taxes. When these people work, they purchase cars and clothing and television sets. Additional hundreds of thousands of people are put to work.

But these jobs are no substitute for the basic program, the Guaranteed Job Opportunity Program.

Who Benefits from a Guaranteed Job Opportunity Program?

Almost everyone.

The jobless who have new hope. Even if they were the only beneficiaries, that alone is worth the effort. The United States cannot hope to regain its momentum in world economic competition with a sizable portion of our population non-productive, non-particapatory and increasingly dissatisfied. Greater participation and contribution by the economically lower one-fifth will not happen unless it is planned, any more than we will be able to compete in any other way with the rest of the world unless we plan and work for it. An article in *Atlantic Monthly* on life in a West Side ghetto of Chicago concluded that a jobs program is the only hope. The author observed: "The great advantage of such a program is that it would enter the lives of ghetto kids when they were eighteen or nineteen and would affect them at a time when most still feel more hopeful than resigned, even if some have been overwhelmed by the traumas of growing up in the ghetto. . . . It is not a wacky scheme requiring a departure from the whole American political system; it is something that America has already done once. It worked and, just as important, it is widely remembered as having worked."[9]

If we put forward this program, the minorities within our central cities will not be the only beneficiaries. Other, less visible, groups also will benefit. For example, the Guaranteed Job Opportunity Program would be a startling lift to many Native Americans living on reservations. Another example would be people who live in the desperately poor, isolated, rural communities across the nation.

Employers will benefit through the increased economic activity that will be generated. They will also experience appreciably lower unemployment compensation costs.

When a Guaranteed Job Opportunity Program is in place, money will be fed into areas that currently are severely depressed, such as East St. Louis, Illinois. That money will not only make life better for those immediate beneficiaries but will also permit grocery stores and clothing shops and other businesses to grow and expand their employment. Businesses will benefit.

The program will encourage greater stress on educational attainment, good for those involved, good for the nation.

States and municipalities will benefit through reduced welfare costs.

Unions will benefit through increased membership generated by: 1) The increased economic activity; 2) Employment of supervisory personnel, many of whom will be union members; and 3) The structural programs that accompany the Guaranteed Job Opportunity Program. For example, the telephone project will create jobs for the International Brotherhood of Electrical Workers and the Commmunications Workers of America.

The Social Security system will be strengthened. The Social Security retirement system had to be buttressed a few years ago for two reasons: unemployment and inflation. Offering the chance to work to millions of Americans who are not working, will eliminate one of the two threats to Social Security.

Reduced crime helps all citizens and assists budgets of governmental units at every level. One writer notes, ''One advantage [of a jobs program] is that criminals can be treated as criminals, without residual guilt about the availability of jobs.''[10] Offer people—particularly young people—an opportunity to earn money rather than steal money, and many will seize that opportunity.

All across the nation, citizens will benefit through projects that improve their communities.

We Can Learn from Experience

It may be trite, but it is true: We don't need to reinvent the wheel. That applies to a jobs program.

In the 1930s this nation had a huge unemployment problem, but fortunately had leadership with the wisdom to understand that you should turn the liability of unemployment into a national asset. That leadership did it with a program called the Works Progress Administration (WPA). People cracked jokes about those working for WPA, about their always leaning on shovels or sitting around and talking—and some of that occurred—but there is not a community in this nation over fifty-years-old that is not a better community for what the WPA did. President Franklin D. Roosevelt created the program through executive order in May, 1935, and by December of that year, 2,667,000 people were working in it.

The jokes about WPA workers are all but forgotten, but the good work they did remains. That includes 125,110 buildings, such as schools and libraries and park lodges built or modernized; 651,000 miles of highways built or improved; 16,100 miles of water line put in; and 24,300 miles of sewer line installed. Hot lunch programs were started in schools where the poor were concentrated. More than 1.5 million adult Americans were taught how to read and write. Over a period of time, that alone paid for the program. Orchestras were started, state guidebooks written, plays produced. Citizens—formerly unhappy and unemployed—received a small amount of money and (more important) gained the satisfaction that they were contributing to a better community and nation. And contribute they did!

Fifty-one years later the times are different, but we still live in a land rich with the potential of these unemployed people and loaded with things that need to be done. Jobs will have to be geared to women much more than they were in 1935. Participants in the WPA were, overwhelmingly, men. Both unions and businesses are better organized than they were in 1935, and some of the projects would have to be handled differently today. But we could teach many more than the 1.5 million adult Americans that the WPA taught to read and write; we could help day care centers; we could develop parks and playgrounds; we could assist in recreational programs for the handicapped; we could help develop industrial parks; we could plant 200 million trees a year. The list can go on and on. There is no shortage of needs; there is no shortage of personnel. What we have a shortage of is creative and courageous political leadership.

In commenting on the WPA programs, Juel Drake, president of the Iron Workers Union, observes: "It's a sad commentary on the state of things that almost nothing done in the jobs and public works area in the half-century since [the WPA] has come close to making such a lasting contribution to our national economy."[11] This union leader concludes, "We need a strategy to provide a good, economically productive job to every man and woman who needs and wants one."

President Roosevelt also started the Civilian Conservation Corps (CCC) for work in the nation's forests. Signed on March 31, 1983, by June 16 of the same year, 239,644 young men had enrolled for almost no pay except for their room and board, all of them sons of welfare recipients or veterans of World War I. No women were in the program. FDR biographer Ted Morgan describes the program: "They were split up in 1,330 work camps located in all the states except Delaware. For many of them it was their first job. They built lookout towers and telephone lines and truck trails and ranger stations. They planted millions of trees. In Wyoming they put out a coal-mine fire that had been burning for seventy years. . . . Tens of thousands were taught to read and write, and thousands went on to college. Many passed civil service exams and joined the forest and national parks services."[12] For a small investment, the nation received tremendous benefits.

The National Youth Administration (NYA) of the FDR administration was similar in concept but, generally, did not move people from their homes. These youths worked in a variety of fields, some of their most lasting contributions made in encouraging young artists and writers.

Public employment experiments with AFDC recipients, with ex-drug addicts and with ex-convicts all point to the public employment alternative as a successful way to lift people, as a wise investment.

Then why don't we do something about it?

The answer is political. When you help people who particularly need a helping hand, the results are not uniformly favorable. One of the reasons some people are down economically is that they are poor managers. When you're dealing with homemakers who have not held a paying job for twenty years, with people who have served time in prison, with people who have had a struggle with alcohol, with people who have not learned to work—with a host of others who could be mentioned—some of them are not going to turn out to be success stories. Newspapers will run articles about some person who abused a program, perhaps we will see a shot on television of some people loafing on the job. So the political leader, in order to avoid being identified with the abuse of a program, tolerates a much greater abuse: using taxpayers' money to pay people for being nonproductive, abusing the least fortunate by not giving them a chance to be useful members of our society.

This is not to suggest that only the most desperate or the poor managers are unemployed and would be participants in the program. When a plant or mine suddenly closes or reduces its work force—often because of imports—many find themselves unable to get employment. They are citizens who have paid their taxes regularly with little or no complaint and who have accumulated enough in limited savings to be ineligible for welfare. They deserve something more than being pushed into poverty before they are helped. A 1986 report on unemployment notes: "Millions of American workers are losing their jobs each year because of structural changes in the U. S. and world economies. Some . . . remain out of work for months, even years. Many of the displaced are middle-aged unskilled or semiskilled manufacturing workers, with long and stable job histories. Mechanisms for worker adjustment . . . have not kept up."[13]

Harry Hopkins, who helped direct the WPA during the 1930s, summed it up well: "Work relief costs more than direct relief but the cost is justified. First, in the saving of morale. Second, in the preservation and creation of human skills and talents. Third, in the material enrichment which the unemployed add to our national wealth through their labors."[14]

Smaller public works projects measures have been enacted through the years, and among those showing leadership on these have been Senators Gaylord Nelson of Wisconsin, Robert Kennedy and Jacob Javits of New York, and Congressmen Augustus Hawkins of California and James Scheuer of New York.

For several years we had the Comprehensive Employment and

Training Act, better known as CETA, under which we provided jobs for hundreds of thousands of Americans who needed those jobs. They were paid little, but the program was modestly successful in raising earnings, especially for women and others with little experience in the job market. Because it was not project-oriented as the Guaranteed Job Opportunity Program is, it aroused opposition from the governmental unions who feared substitution, and experienced some of it, as well as the more traditional forces that oppose any move to help people in need. But that combination of opposition to CETA proved fatal. There was some abuse—abuse that cannot be defended—and, unfortunately, some substitution because workers were simply assigned to a governmental unit rather than on a project basis as suggested in the Guaranteed Job Opportunity Program. Instead of correcting the wrongs and keeping what was good in the program, CETA was killed. Killing it was good politics but bad public policy.

CETA was succeeded by JTPA, a program that is more popular than CETA in part because of the lessons learned from some of CETA's mistakes, but in part because JTPA has been more selective in choosing people to serve. JTPA, for example, so far has served 18 percent fewer people who had not finished high school than did CETA, but has served 10.8 percent more of those who were high school graduates.[15] Pick those to serve carefully, and the results will improve; there will be fewer public relations disasters.

But those who have not graduated from high school are more likely to be the people in great need. For example, often the person now employed under the JTPA program for displaced workers is someone who already has skills and some motivation. That is not to detract from the program. It is good. The 5 percent of eligibles they now reach generally are the more promising potential employees. Understandably. You want results; the program demands results. But the person who has been out of work some time who is less skilled, less motivated, and less buoyant of spirit is the more difficult person to place. The other part of JTPA for the disadvantaged workers helps but could help more. The total amount spent on federal job training and employment programs was approximatley one-third as much in Fiscal Year 1985 as in Fiscal Year 1979. The other difference between the two is that JTPA participants are more likely to be male. The CETA program, particularly the public service portion of it, had a higher percentage of female participation.

But the Guaranteed Job Opportunity Program is not designed to take the place of JTPA. JTPA should serve all it can, but those not served by JTPA and other programs—the millions who now fall through the cracks—should have better alternatives than signing up for welfare or impoverishment or crime. The Guaranteed Job Opportunity Program will give them a chance.

WPA, CCC, NYA, CETA and other experiments have shown us what can be done.

In the 1930s, Illinois had a remarkable congressman, Kent E. Keller, who in 1936 wrote a book *Prosperity Through Employment.* Its basic message is as current as when it was written half a century ago. Among his observations:

— ''We are confronted with...whether we can permit widespread poverty as a result of widespread unemployment and deny opportunity in the very midst of opulence, and still retain our present form of government.''[16]

— ''The large manufacturers watch in vain for the abundant orders that a population at work invariably brings.''[17]

— ''Every hour wasted in enforced idleness is irretrievably lost to the service of mankind.''[18]

— ''This depression can be fully ended only by providing jobs. The return of depressions can be prevented only by making jobs permanent.''[19]

— ''The average span of life [in England] of the so-called 'working class' was only twenty-three years.... The average life span today is fifty-eight years, and scientists assert that with living conditions now available the average may reach seventy-six.''[20]

— "It is so easy for a man who has the power, to decide an issue in his own favor.... And where there is a great body of men with similar interests and with full power to decide, the power of such concentrated interest becomes irresistible, producing a defensive argument warped and biased beyond all reason, blind to truth, contemptuous of justice."[21]

— "From the very beginning up to the present time, every economic and social abuse yet corrected, has been corrected by law, and only by law."[22]

— "Without government the final result has always been that the strong in effect devoured the weak."[23]

— "These millions of unemployed are flesh of our flesh.... Our first duty is to relieve their present suffering, to make certain that they be never again subjected to such ignominy."[24]

— "Everyone should know this very simple fact.... Put all the idle men to work—keep them at work—and business will thrive."[25]

— "America is going to pay out money for work or for idleness. We must make our choice."[26]

— "We must accept as our national policy the duty of government to guarantee universal employment—a job for every man and woman who wants to work.... This is the one requirement that is absolutely necessary to the retention of the capitalistic system and to the form of government dependent on that system.... Any plan that falls short of creating and maintaining 'a job for every man and woman who wants to work' will fail. All other proposals are incidental to carrying out this one vital national policy."[27]

— "It costs the nation more to keep men idle than it does to keep them at work. Yes, it actually costs more in dollars and cents to pauperize a man, than to let him freely and joyously create wealth."[28]

Kent Keller was right!

We should dare to do something almost unprecedented: learn from history.

Encouraging the Private Sector

The Guaranteed Job Opportunity Program is not a substitute for doing everything possible to encourage the private sector to provide employment. I believe in the free enterprise system but the private sector by itself is not able to provide all the jobs that need to be created. It should, however, be encouraged to provide as many as possible.

JTPA helps on this. It takes people who are out of work and have been out of work a significant amount of time, and gives an incentive to an employer to hire them. An example is Abbott Products, a small manufacturing company in Chicago operated by Nelson Carlo.

He has been able to take advantage of the JTPA program to help his business and help the unemployed. They work for him while they are being trained. Many stay and work for him permanently and some, he admits with a grin, leave after training and go to work for larger companies where they can make more money. While they work for him and receive training, he receives 25 percent of their pay from the federal government—an inducement to employ people who after more than six months away from any job are less and less employable. It is good for him, for the employees, and for the federal government.

Experiments unrelated to any present program should be carried out with other less cumbersome options to encourage private job placement of those who have been out of the work force for a long period. For example, those unemployed more than sixty days might be given simple vouchers, entitling an employer to reimbursement for a set amount per hour for a period of months for employing that person. Opponents argue that if the market conditions are right, the employer will hire people, and if they're wrong, they won't no matter what the voucher system or other incentive. There is some truth to that, but the truth is limited. The short-term unemployed are more likely to find employment on their own.

Other ideas should be tried. The nation has fifty laboratories called states. We should try new ideas to encourage private sector participation in placement of the longer-term unemployed. For the most part, business leaders want to demonstrate good citizenship, but those same leaders also have a responsiblity to show profits. If we can devise more and better methods of providing assistance without diminishing profits, much more of the business world will join the effort.

Before Frank Lautenberg became a member of the United States Senate from New Jersey, he served as chief executive officer of Automatic Data Processing, which employs 18,000 people. His company took some people who were on welfare and taught them basic skills, conveyed why good attitudes are important, and taught them how to fill out job applications. The turnover of this small group of welfare recipients hired into the firm has not been greater than that of other employees. One of those former welfare recipients is now a supervisor.

Automatic Data Processing did itself a favor and did our society a favor. Private sector contributions need to be encouraged on a much broader scale.

But enlisting the support of the private sector is not a substitute for the new safety net the nation needs: a Guaranteed Job Opportunity Program.

A Slight Help on Income Distribution

We are quietly, undramatically but unquestionably creating some long-range problems for ourselves through a shift in income distribution. In the last few years I have heard a growing—still small but growing—number of speeches that pit class against class, leaving me with an unsettled feeling that something basic to the nation is coming unglued.

Even a 1986 report from the Joint Economic Committee of Congress divides wealth in the nation into four categories: the super rich, the very rich, the rich, and everyone else.

It is not hard to find the source of our problems. During the past decade, the top 10 percent of our population has shown growth in income, the bottom 90 percent loss. For the first time since the Great Depression, we have a shrinking percentage of Americans owning their own homes, a smaller percentage belonging to the legendary middle class. The difference in average income from the top 10 percent of our population to the bottom 10 percent in the United States is fourteen to one. In West Germany the person in the top 10 percent has only six times as much income as those in the bottom 10 percent, and in Japan an even smaller difference. In 1969, the middle 50 percent of our population (third through seventh decile) had 39 percent of the income. By 1982, it had dropped to 34 percent, and it is still shrinking.

Unfortunately the massive overhaul of the tax code completed in the fall of 1986 will widen the gap between the more fortunate and the less fortunate. The more fortunate are much better lobbyists than the less fortunate!

Labor unions performed a major role in creating a healthy middle class, but as manufacturing slipped from 36 percent of private employment in 1965 to 24 percent in 1985, the power and numbers of labor unions also slipped. Manufacturing as a percentage of our gross national product has been fairly constant since the Korean War, but in part because of the cooperation of progressive labor unions—and in part because of flawed trade policies—employment in manufacturing has been decreasing dramatically.

The United States today has a substantially smaller percentage of workers unionized than most democratic countries. The combination of the massive loss of jobs due to imports and the decline in power of the unions has resulted in growing numbers of poor and a shrinking middle class. The appointees of the Reagan administration to the National Labor Relations Board have made that body the most anti-union NLRB in history, and its rulings have reflected that strong bias. Traditionally, under both Democratic and Republican administrations, the NLRB has been fairly even-handed, without too much of a tilt toward either labor or management. That shift under the Reagan administration is an additional cause of loss of union membership. Some European labor leaders believe that U. S. labor unions have much less of a society perspective, resulting in a higher ratio of strikes per man hour here, and a public reluctant to look favorably on unions. But those who view the decline of labor unions as a healthy development may awaken some morning to find sizable numbers of American workers demanding much more radical alternatives. The inevitable result of a widening gap between rich and poor will be a radicalization and polarization that can only mean serious upheavals at some future point if the trend is not stopped.

New Jersey is the third wealthiest state in the nation in per capita income. But it has the city over 100,000 with the lowest per capita income, Newark, and the city between 50,000 and 100,000 with the lowest per capita income, Camden. Newark, with a population of 350,000, does not have a movie theater. New Jersey symbolizes the nation's problem.

A 1986 study published by the Joint Economic Committee of Congress reported a growing concentration of wealth in this nation. The report also noted that the "long-term trend in declining concentration of wealth, which began with the 1929 stock-market crash, continued through the early to mid-1970s. . . . The dramatic increase in the share of national wealth held by the richest Americans . . . did not begin until late in the [1963-1983] period."[29] Since the publication of this study, some of the precise statistics it reported have been questioned, but no one questions the validity of the assumption on the trends.

A Guaranteed Job Opportunity Program does not solve all the problems of income and wealth distribution, but it reduces them slightly. Even at the present minimum wage level, the numbers living below the poverty level would be reduced under the Guaranteed Job Opportunity Program, and the opportunity for many to move up the economic ladder would be increased.

Assuming that the minimum wage is increased perhaps thirty cents an hour during the next administration, whether Democratic or Republican, under the Guaranteed Job Opportunity Program that would further modestly reduce the huge disparity between the most fortunate and the least fortunate in our society. And that increase in the minimum wage is overdue. Since the last increase in the minimum wage in 1981, inflation has caused a decline in its effective rate of 26 percent. In non-inflationary terms, relative to the rest of the economy, the minimum wage is now at its lowest level since 1955. While a thirty-cent-an-hour increase in the minimum wage may not seem important to many readers, to those struggling to get by on a minimum wage, that extra twelve dollars a week (for forty hours) can make a huge difference.

The wisdom in avoiding a society with too many poor and a few very wealthy is not some profound truth that suddenly descended on humanity. Four hundred years before Christ, Plato wrote, "There should exist among the citizens neither extreme poverty, nor, again, excess of wealth for both are productive of evils."[30] And fourteen years before the Declaration of Independence, Jean Jacques Rousseau observed, "Allow neither rich men nor beggars. These two estates...are equally fatal to the common good; from the one come the friends of tyranny, and from the other tyrants. It is always between them that public liberty is put at auction; the one buys, the other sells."[31] Both Plato and Rousseau wrote before any country had developed the large middle-income group that this nation first developed. So long as there is that sizable middle income group a society can tolerate those with great wealth; in fact those with wealth serve as a stimulus and model for hard work and creativity and risk-taking. But at some point if the people of limited means become too numerous and feel put upon, then a society has an explosive situation. Writing from France, Thomas Jefferson told James Madison of the concentration of wealth "in a very few hands" with long-term consequences that would not be good for France.[32] He hoped that our nation could avoid that danger. He might well have been writing to us today.

However, the main reason for supporting a Guaranteed Job Opportunity Program should not be to avoid political explosions in the future. We should favor it because it makes sense for the economy of the nation, and it is humanitarian. But the program also is prudent insurance for the future of our political system, and we should develop a sense of urgency about providing that insurance. You would not drive your car without automobile insurance because of what might happen. We should not drive our government without protection for the unemployed, both because of humanitarian reasons and because of what could happen to the system.

Franklin D. Roosevelt once said, "The test of our progress is not whether we add more to the abundance of those who have much; it is whether we provide enough for those who have too little."[33]

Endnotes

1. Editorial, "The Cost of Chronic Poverty," *Chicago Tribune,* Dec. 23, 1984.

2. *Economic Justice for All,* Third Draft (Washington: National Conference of Catholic Bishops, 1986), p. 39.

3. Patrick J. McDonough, Executive Director, American Association for Counseling and Development, from statement accompanying letter to Paul Simon, Jan. 24, 1986.

4. The Report of the Committee on Federalism and National Purpose, *To Form a More Perfect Union* (Washington: National Conference on Social Welfare, 1985), p. xi.

5. Gary Orfield, quoted in "Brother Can You Spare a Job?" by Alfredo S. Lanier, *Chicago,* September 1985.

6. Social Security Administration *Quarterly Public Assistance Statistics,* "Table 13.—AFDC: Families, recipients, and payments, by State, April 1985."

7. Institute for Development of Education Activities and the National Association of Elementary School Principals, *The Most Significant Minority: One-Parent Children in the Schools* (Alexandria, VA: National Association of Elementary School Principals, 1980), pp. 8; 9; 16.

8. George W. Norris, quoted in *The Persistence of a Progressive,* by Richard Lowitt (Urbana: University of Illinois Press, 1974), p. 494.

9. "The Origins of the Underclass," by Nicholas Lemann, *The Atlantic Monthly,* July 1986.

10. "The Work Ethic State," by Mickey Kaus, *The New Republic,* July 7, 1986.

11. Juel D. Drake, General President, International Association of Bridge, Structural and Ornamental Iron Workers, letter to Paul Simon, Jan. 24, 1986.

12. Ted Morgan, *FDR: A Biography* (New York: Simon and Schuster, 1985), p. 380.

13. Report Brief, Office of Technology Assessment, U. S. Congress, "Technology and Structural Unemployment: Reemploying Displaced Adults," Feb. 1986.

14. Quoted in Milton Meltzer, *Violins and Shovels* (New York: Delacorte Press, 1976), p. 18.

15. Gary Orfield and Helene Slessarev, *Job Training Under the New Federalism* (Chicago: University of Chicago, 1986), p. 107.

16. Kent E. Keller, *Prosperity Through Employment* (New York: Harper and Brothers, 1936), p. 5.

17. *Ibid*, p. 10.

18. *Ibid*, p. 11.

19. *Ibid*, p. 13.

20. *Ibid*, pp. 34 and 232.

21. *Ibid*, p. 55.

22. *Ibid*, pp. 67 and 68.

23. *Ibid*, p. 114.

24. *Ibid*, p. 164.

25. *Ibid*, p. 172.

26. *Ibid*, p. 174.

27. *Ibid*, p. 214.

28. *Ibid*, p. 228.

29. "The Concentration of Wealth in the United States," by the Democratic Staff of the Joint Economic Committee, published by the Joint Economic Committee, United States Congress, July 1986, pp. 10-43.

30. Plato, *Dialogues of Plato*, Laws V., *Great Books* (Chicago: Encyclopedia Britannica, 1952), Vol. 7, p. 695.

31. Jean Jacques Rousseau, *The Social Contract in Great Books* (Chicago: Encyclopedia Britannica, 1952), Vol. 38, p. 405.

32. Thomas Jefferson, letter to James Madison, Oct. 28, 1785, *Papers of Thomas Jefferson,* edited by Julian P. Boyd, Vol. VIII (Princeton, NJ: Princeton University Press, 1953), pp. 681-683.

33. Caroline Thomas Harnsberger, Editor, *Treasury of Presidential Quotations* (Chicago: Follett, 1964), p. 255.

SECTION THREE

PUTTING THE ANSWERS TO WORK

Chapter Five

How Much Will It Cost?

An IMMEDIATE RETORT to the question that heads this chapter is: What will it cost *not* to do it? The costs in not doing it are beyond calculation in wasted humanity, in keeping this nation from moving toward a more creative and productive and competitive tomorrow, in needlessly dividing the nation more and more into two camps: those who have a job and home and car on one side, and on the other side, the less fortunate who find themselves more and more alienated.

But answering a question with a negative is not answering it completely. There are realistic fiscal considerations when you launch an enterprise significantly changing the way we handle one of our major social problems.

Costs cannot be figured precisely, but it is possible to make an approximation.

If we were to raise everyone above the poverty level, just handing people checks, the cost would be $46 billion. While that is a huge sum, it is approximately 4.5 percent of the federal budget. Or to use another comparison, the increase in the defense budget authority requested by President Reagan for fiscal year 1987 was $31 billion. Take that and add 50 percent, and you have the total to eliminate poverty in this country simply by handing people checks.

I do not advocate simply handing people more money. Such an answer would cause serious social problems. It would discourage rather than encourage productivity. In the long run it would do harm to our desperate need to face up to the competitive world in which we now find ourselves. It also does not offer people the chance to feel they are contributing something to society, a satisfaction that all citizens ought to be able to experience.

But even this approach of simply handing people money to eliminate poverty is within the budgetary possibilities of this nation.

To estimate the cost of a better answer, let us look at the numbers and the programs:

Official number of unemployed	8,000,000
Official number of "discouraged workers"	1,200,000
People working so little part-time that they are almost unemployed	800,000
TOTAL	10,000,000
Out of work less than five weeks, therefore, ineligible for this job program	3,360,000
	6,640,000

Half of those covered by unemployment
compensation who will not want to join in
the jobs program, 935,000 minus 100,000
overlap under the five-week exclusion   835,000

5,805,000

Infrastructure job program (highways,
telephones, sewers, etc.) outlined in previous
chapter   500,000

That leaves approximately five million people unemployed to
be covered by this program. If sound fiscal, trade and education
policies advocated in chapter 3 are followed, that figure should
drop by as much as two million. But let us assume that does not
happen.

During the Works Progress Administration (WPA) program of
a half-century ago, three million out of a total of nine million unemployed participated. For a variety of reasons—including moving from one place to another, or the sense that another job would
break for them soon—most people are not likely to take advantage of the program.

Assume that three million of the five million enter into the program (a high figure), at an average wage slightly above the minimum because of the 10-percent-plus feature that some will have.
Let us say that the average annual pay is $6,000 and that the total
administrative and equipment and supply costs are $2,000 per job
filled. That administrative cost is somewhat high because it includes the employer's, that is, the federal government's, contribution to Social Security of $429 a year. That would be a gross cost
of $24 billion.

If the same proportion take these jobs as during the WPA days,
that would be 1,700,000 jobs, or a gross cost of $13.6 billion.
The job figure could be lower than that, close to one million—the
estimate of one economist who looked over the proposal—for a
cost of $8 billion. But to be fiscally prudent, let us assume the
highest gross cost figure, $24 billion.

President Reagan uses the figure that each 1 percent of unemployment costs the federal government $28 billion. Since removing three million people from the unemployment roles reduces unemployment almost 3 percent, there is at least the possibility that the program will save money, not be a cost.

But for the moment, forget this 1 percent-equals-$28 billion measure because that measurement assumes not only the burden side of the equation, it also assumes that those employed will pay income taxes, which few of the three million in this program will do at their reentry jobs.

For fiscal purposes, when a federal budget is put together, the general assumption is made that a one dollar expenditure will return approximately 25 cents. This varies from program to program, but when one dollar is spent on a farm program, for example, the farmer increases his or her taxes paid a little, buys more at the local hardware store and farm implement dealer whose owners pay more taxes. The end result is not that the federal government gets all its money back, but it does receive, on the average, approximately twenty-five cents on each dollar spent on programs. Using that assumption, the $24 billion is reduced to $18 billion. Savings in welfare and unemployment compensation should save an additional significant amount. Federal government outlays for Fiscal Year 1986 included $19.8 billion for unemployment compensation, $9.2 billion for AFDC, $11.7 billion for food stamps, and $24.5 billion for Medicaid. If you assume that this program would result in a drop of one-third in unemployment compensation, one-third in AFDC, one-fifth in food stamps and one-tenth in Medicaid, the immediate savings would be $14.5 billion. That does not count the savings in prisons and energy assistance and other smaller programs that are less obvious. Let us be ultra-conservative and assume that the total savings are not $14.5 billion—already a conservative figure—but let us bring it down to $10 billion.

Assuming that the savings are $10 billion, the net cost is brought down to $8 billion. That does not count the benefits in reduced crime, educational improvement, and an unmeasurable but significant factor: an improved spirit across the land among the nation's least fortunate. It does not count the increased revenue to the Social Security system. It does not count the savings to states and local governments. A five-year study of the impact of a 1.4 percent increase in unemployment in 1970 reached the conclusion that it had "cost our society nearly $7 billion in lost income due to illness and mortality, and in added state prison and mental hospital outlays."[1] Figuring that it would cost the nation $8 billion—a high figure—to put people to work does not count all of these hidden savings that are not immediately obvious.

And, it does not count the improved communities we will have around the nation.

The $8 billion cost—less than one percent of the federal budget—does not count the infrastructural changes suggested in the previous chapter, changes which we should make whether we go ahead with a Guaranteed Job Opportunity Program or not.

The educational benefits from the Guaranteed Job Opportunity Program will also have significant long-term benefits. Those who apply for the jobs will be screened for literacy and educational needs, and those who need help will be given that help. In the long run, this one provision in itself will more than pay for the Guaranteed Job Opportunity Program. Precise calculations are not possible, but if in the first year of the program, one million of the nation's twenty-three million illiterate are taught to be significantly more self-sufficient, and that results in an average increase of income of $2,000 a year (a low figure), that means a gross total increase in income for them of $2 billion a year. In ten years that is $20 billion, and if the tax on that additional income is 15 percent, the direct return to the federal government is $3 billion. Add that to their increased productivity for the nation, and the increased likelihood that their children will perform better and that there will be other indirect spinoffs from this, and this one small but important part of the program will eventually pay for the total program—and that does not count the many other benefits to our society.

Perhaps more important than literacy and the academically elevating features that will be part of this program is the education people receive by doing—generally the most effective educational tool. People learn not only a skill, but showing up for work regularly and on time.

Those who say that the Guaranteed Job Opportunity Program will save more in welfare, unemployment compensation, prison outlays and other expenditures than it will cost may be correct. No one can know for sure. But if at the outside we must spend $8 billion—one fourth of the *increase* requested for the 1987 defense budget—it will be the best investment we can make.

When the economy is up, the costs of this program will be down. The President should have flexibility in implementing the program. We do not need a rigid three million jobs filled. The program need not start going full-blast. If it were to start with certain preferences, the program could reach everyone in two or even three years. There are over 500,000 unemployed Vietnam veterans who could receive priority consideration. People who are the sole income for a family—primarily women—could be given preference. Any number of options exist. But as rapidly as possible, all eligible people should be offered a job opportunity.

A serious look at our economy shows that for the immediate decades ahead, even when the macroeconomic indicators are good, there will be a softness in the economy for our underclass. The vessel christened U. S. S. Healthy Economy does not bring millions of citizens aboard. It should.

But Won't Such a Plan Be Inflationary?

No. It is inflationary to pay people for doing nothing, not for being productive. It is inflationary to have sizable segments of a population not learning good work habits. The traditional definition of inflation is "too much money chasing too few goods." If people are non-productive, or less productive than they should be, there are fewer goods produced, and prices rise. If, for example, there are ten watches produced, and there is $100 in circulation, each watch will cost $10. One way of having inflation is to produce ten watches but print more money. If you have $120 in circulation (instead of $100), each watch will cost $12. But another way of having inflation is to keep the same amount of money in circulation, but produce fewer watches. Then the price of watches rises. When people are not productive, it is inflationary.

In pure economic theory there should be no such thing as unemployment, for the classical law of supply and demand should adjust to the employment market, and everyone who wants work should be employed. In pure economic theory a sensible way to slow inflation is through decreased demand for employment. Both of these economic theories look good in a textbook or on a blackboard but do not look so good when applied to life. In real life, these theories come down to slowing inflation by creating misery in the lives of millions of families.

It is true that one of the ways a nation can slow inflation is by increasing unemployment, but it is not the only way, and it is not the best way.

Unfortunately, the United States is inching toward eliminating some of the other tools traditionally used to reduce inflation. Perhaps the worst example is our tendency toward more and more indexation—raising expenditures as the cost of living goes up—of everything from retirement programs to tax rates. Indexation is, in and of itself, inflationary, and we compound our problem literally by compounding the inflation rate. Unfortunately, indexation is as popular as it is unwise. Israel and Brazil are the classic examples of indexing gone amok. But the temptation to use indexing is there for politicians in every country, and the United States is gradually getting into that quicksand. It becomes easy for the politician to say to specific groups, "I'm protecting your interests." As more and more is indexed, the public is protected less and less. One of the little-noted results of indexing is that it forces an administration to look at the tool of unemployment to resist inflation. Economist Lester Thurow has observed, "Whatever the level of unemployment necessary to control inflation in an unindexed world, it is clear that level is much higher in an indexed world.''[2]

While the current indexation limits alternatives in controlling inflation and makes higher unemployment more likely, even with indexation we can have full employment and virtually no inflation, though it is more difficult. As you look to post-World War II economic history, one of the striking parallels is that with two exceptions, when unemployment goes down, so does inflation. Let people be productive, and the price of the goods produced generally will stay down. The Guaranteed Job Opportunity Plan gives people the chance to be productive.

In economic terms, the most successful presidency in this century was that of Harry S. Truman. Taking the post-war years 1947-1953, his administration experienced economic growth of 4.8 percent per year. Unemployment averaged 4 percent and reached 2.9 percent his final year, and the total deficit for Fiscal Years 1947 through 1953—using today's calculating methods— was $640 million, or less than $100 million a year. This is an incredible performance when you consider these were post-war years with some unusual expenditures and that during these years we fought in a war in Korea. The man who chaired President Truman's Council of Economic Advisers, Leon H. Keyserling, recently testified before a House subcommittee. He noted that ''more idle plants and more unemployment mean more inflation.'' He called for development of federal programs and policies ''based on experience as well as reason, which move toward achievement of the best instead of acceptance of the worst. . . . Federal policies should be integrated, coherent, and long-range, not random, improvised and often inconsistent. . . . Our national economic policies are bent upon compounding failures instead of generating successes. We are becoming a nation of what we 'cannot afford,' instead of a nation dedicated to what we can and must do. We surrender to what is going wrong, and actual national policies aggravate what is going wrong, instead of reversing the process to get things to go right. We attempt Maginot lines against adverse forces, instead of marshalling a pro-prosperity advance.''[3]

Ultimately, ''marshalling a pro-prosperity advance'' is much less costly and less inflationary than drifting aimlessly, hoping that somehow the free market forces will automatically create a better tomorrow for everyone. The evidence of history is that if you assume reasonably prudent monetary and fiscal policies, if you let people be productive, the net result is *de*flationary, not *in*flationary.

After World War II, inflation threatened Western Europe, because there was so little to purchase in those war-devastated economies. One of the little-heralded victories of the Marshall Plan was to stop inflation by a generous supply of consumer goods. It worked. What works in Western Europe works everywhere: Increase the supply of goods through increased productivity, and you slow inflation.

But Will People Be Paid Enough?

Some of the critics to whom I have shown this proposal have suggested that the basic pay should be higher. Many people will not be lifted above poverty, they argue. There are several answers to that.

First, the pay should be low enough so that the incentive is present to encourage people to move from the Guaranteed Job Opportunity Program into a private sector job. Under this proposal, everyone eligible will make more money than they now draw being non-productive; but anyone willing to work and able to find a job in the private sector for forty hours a week, rather than thirty-two hours a week under this program, will make an additional 25 percent in income.

Second, as you raise the pay level, you raise the cost, and you increase the likelihood the program cannot pass Congress.

Two recent in-depth articles on the problems of the nation's poor and unemployed—one by Mickey Kaus in *The New Republic* and one by Nicholas Lemann in *The Atlantic Monthly*—both suggest a guaranteed jobs program as the only possible cure for the nation's growing underclass problem. I agree with them on that but both suggest pay below the minimum wage as a way to encourage those working to get private-sector jobs.

I appreciate their desire to encourage private sector jobs, but my proposal provides that, through the thirty-two-hour-a-week provision, rather than forty hours a week. Paying below the minimum wage will not give people the lift they need. Paying them above the minimum wage, with the few exceptions noted earlier, will not encourage them enough to get off the government payroll. This proposal strikes a sensible balance.

A Possible Cost Factor: The Draft

For much of the next decade there will be a gradually shrinking pool of personnel in the age group that ordinarily composes the bulk of the enlistees in the armed services. This age group also has high unemployment rates, particularly among blacks and Hispanics. Whatever decision is made on the draft will have a major impact on the unemployment picture. A draft would lower the unemployment rate and the costs of the Guaranteed Job Opportunity Program substantially.

Those who believe the emphasis of the armed forces should be nuclear see no danger in a declining number of armed service personnel.

The other side believes that we must maintain a sufficient nuclear deterrence so that there is no miscalculation by the Soviets, but that the principle need for the armed forces will be to respond quickly and effectively with conventional means, to put out "brush fires." We should send a solid signal to any would-be aggressor that the United States has the ability to act, and has options other than nuclear options. This side sees personnel shortages ahead.

I find myself in the latter camp.

The demographic factors will cause more and more discussion about some kind of compulsory military service. If it comes—

and it is at least a 50/50 possibility—I shall strongly oppose the type of draft we had during the Vietnam War with its college deferments. That resulted in the bloodshed in Vietnam being primarily that of the children of the poor.

If we get to the point of considering a draft, I shall push for something along this line: All males (Congress has overwhelmingly rejected even registering females, though I voted for it) must serve their country for one year, following graduation from high school or upon reaching the age of eighteen. Since only one-eighth of that total will be needed in the armed forces, most could serve in some other capacity. If they choose the military, they will get special education benefits upon leaving the service. If they want to work for a park district or mental hospital, help old people in a nursing home, teach people how to read and write, help maintain a museum, repair books in a library, or join the Peace Corps, they can. There will be hundreds of choices, but every draftee must serve one year. Educational tests would be administered to everyone drafted, and those who need special help would be given it. Counseling would be available for all.

Those who favor this idea are from all sides of the political scene: Conservative Columnist William F. Buckley, Jr., Ford Foundation President Franklin Thomas, *Washington Monthly* editor Charles Peters, Democratic Representative Leon Panetta of California.

Polls show that if such a plan were enacted, a much higher percentage of middle and upper income young men would enter the armed forces than now do, because of the post-service education benefits. That is important. I recall when the House was discussing having U. S. military advisers in El Salvador. Representative Clarence Long of Maryland said during the debate that he was the only member of Congress to have a son in Vietnam. It struck me that if we had had more sons—or daughters—of members of Congress in Vietnam, we would have been out of there much sooner. Careless use of military personnel is easier when those who suffer are the children of ''other people.''

But if such a draft comes, it will absorb a sizable pool of the unemployed, reducing the costs of a Guaranteed Job Opportunity Program. It virtually eliminates unemployment among eighteen-year-old males, but it also reduces other unemployment because eighteen-year-old males working would have to be replaced by eighteen-year-old females or nineteen-year-old males or others across the spectrum. It is also possible that if a draft of this form would evolve that the public would find it acceptable for females also; at least some early signs indicate that. If females were included, it would both help the unemployment picture and help women through tests, literacy and education programs, and other measures that would be more available to males than females if such a draft did not include females. What impact a draft would have on unemployment has not been studied carefully because no one knows what final form it may take. Properly shaped, a draft could be helpful in reducing unemployment rates and in meeting the educational deficiencies of millions of young Americans.

Whether there will be a draft probably will not be decided until 1989, shortly after the next president is inaugurated. But the wisdom or cost-effectiveness of a Guaranteed Job Opportunity Program is not dependent on a draft.

An employment program is a good investment no matter what happens on a draft.

But Can a Guaranteed Job Opportunities Program Be Enacted?

Today, no. But soon, yes.

As the idea spreads and groups see they will benefit, the pressure will grow to take this major step forward toward a better society. There is virtually no organized support for it today. It is viewed as some distant, unachievable vision.

The unions, often in the forefront of progress in the nation, will once again have to lead the way. Even the public sector unions that now generally stand opposed to public service jobs can be persuaded to shift their position when they see that there will be no substitution of Guaranteed Job Opportunity Program beneficiaries for their positions. The veto power given in local districts to both union and business representatives should allay those fears.

Businesses that are tired of paying high unemployment compensation bills should gradually be brought aboard, even though their national organizations will probably accept the idea more reluctantly than will the businesses around the nation.

Veterans organizations should support it when they see veterans as major beneficiaries.

Organizations representing the disabled should become major supporters when they understand the life-time safety net a Guaranteed Job Opportunity Program provides. It would benefit the disabled by giving them practical work experiences that too many of them do not have, and it would benefit them in another unusual way: Many employers now are reluctant to hire the disabled because they don't want to be faced with the unpleasant and distasteful possibility of having to fire someone who cannot do the job. If some alternative other than unemployment were available for the disabled, more employers would be willing to take what many now view as a risk.

A number of other groups could be listed as among those potentially willing to actively promote and push for the Guaranteed Job Opportunity Program, but first the seed of the idea has to be planted. As it begins to grow—and people see it growing—more and more people and organizations will come to support it.

If the Guaranteed Job Opportunity Program were brought to the floor of the Senate and House in the fall of 1986, probably one-third of the members would vote for it. We need more votes. But even more we need about five senators and fifteen House members who are solidly committed to work hard for its enactment. Because of all the demands on the time of members that is not a simple request. But if we can find those five senators and fifteen House members—joined by an understanding public—we will see a Guaranteed Job Opportunity Program in this country. You who read these lines can help stimulate that.

No mountain of evidence will convince some that the federal government should do anything substantial to help the less fortunate. The late Senator Paul Douglas wrote, "There is a peculiar group of cynics who always attack attempts to help the poor."[4]

It is ironic that public opinion polls for a change are leading us in the right direction, but we resist. Polls show the majority of the public favors guaranteeing a job opportunity to everyone but opposes a guaranteed income for everyone. Yet we have backed into doing the latter. The income varies from state to state, but the income guarantee is what we now have. We recognize that we cannot be civilized and let people starve, so we have adopted a policy which pays people for doing nothing. If instead we were to adopt a policy of paying people for being productive, we would have the strong backing of public opinion.

What we are doing is substituting words for action on the jobs front. Any candidate or public official can—without advanced preparation—make a resounding speech on how we ought to put people to work. But voting to follow through on the words is much more difficult. A recent study found: "Programs contain promises, but budgets provide resources. . . . Since few states and localities provide their own budgets for employment and training, the federal decisions determine the level of resources available. . . . The budget trends show the impact of the elimination of one major strategy, public service employment. . . . All of this occurred in times of growing joblessness. The result. . . is an extremely sharp reduction in resources per jobless worker."[5]

No one should be fooled. A Guaranteed Job Opportunity Program will cost money. But the benefits from those expenditures are beyond calculation.

Endnotes

1. "Personal Stability and Economic Security," by M. Harvey Brenner, *Social Policy,* May-June 1977.

2. Lester C. Thurow, *The Zero-Sum Solution* (New York: Simon and Schuster, 1985), p. 321.

3. Leon H. Keyserling, Testimony before the House Subcommittee on Education and Labor, Sept. 4, 1985.

4. Paul H. Douglas, *In the Fullness of Time: The Memoirs of Paul H. Douglas* (New York: Harcourt Brace Jovanovich, 1974), p. 402.

5. Gary Orfield and Helene Slessarev, *Job Training Under the New Federalism* (Chicago: University of Chicago, 1986), p.61.

Chapter Six

Leadership by the States

GOVERNOR MICHAEL S. DUKAKIS of Massachusetts
is one of several state chief executives who has offered innova-
tion to the nation, a laboratory of a program that works. Far different and far more limited than the Guaranteed Job Opportunity
Program, it is called the Massachusetts Employment and Training (ET) Choices program.

Under the ET Choices program 23,000 welfare recipients have
been placed in full-time or part-time work with 6,000 businesses.
No direct subsidy is given to the business, other than having received an employee who has been well trained.

Under ET Choices, welfare recipients have four alternatives:

— Assessment and Career Counseling
— Education and Training

— On-the-Job Training Through Supported Work
— Direct Job Placement

People can go from one program to another. Many, for example, feel they need the assessment and counseling before they can opt for one of the other alternatives.

Those who contract with the state to train people have to place them in jobs paying more than $5.00 per hour, otherwise there is no state payment to the contractor.

The program has been a success. Governor Dukakis and the legislature of Massachusetts have every reason to boast of their program.

But...

Massachusetts has an unemployment rate of 3.9 percent, a drop from 12.3 percent in 1975. More than 50,000 new businesses have come to the state in the last two years. Massachusetts is booming. The New England region has an unemployment rate of 4.5 percent, compared to a 12 percent rate in 1975. Critics argue that this healthy economic environment is responsible for many of the 23,000 jobs placed. They argue that to really know the impact of this program, you should have two control groups, one of which is helped by the ET program and one of which is not. Then you can learn what "net" employment gain there is.

It is unlikely that Governor Dukakis is going to be moved by his critics. The reality is that if the "net" figure is 23,000 or 10,000 or 5,000, creative state leadership has helped.

Would the Dukakis program be as successful in a state like Illinois, with almost 10 percent unemployment? It is doubtful. It would be a good program in any state, but part of the dramatic success is the environment in which it functions.

In Massachusetts the Guaranteed Job Opportunity Program would back up the state program and would replace some of the welfare assistance. But if the entire nation were as healthy economically as Massachusetts, I would not be writing this book. The average welfare recipient in Massachusetts receives $400 per month. Under the Guaranteed Job Opportunity Program the pay would be $464 per month plus what could be earned in private employment, part-time. The average pay for those hired full-time in the private sector under the ET Choices program is $841 a month.

California has embarked on the most complex employment and training program for welfare recipients, and it will be two years or longer before the results can be measured. A bipartisan coalition was put together by Assemblyman Art Agnos to produce overwhelming passage of Greater Avenues for Independence, with the acronym GAIN. Governor George Deukmejian signed the measure into law. A system of counseling and training, together with practical incentives for people to search for jobs, makes it a promising experiment, though women with children under six are not required to participate—and that is more than 50 percent of the welfare cases.

Again, California does not have the unemployment problem that plagues many other states. When I asked Assemblyman Agnos what they do if jobs are not available and they cannot place people, he had no answer. Politically he and the others determined that if they had included a public service job feature in the plan, it would have jeopardized all of their good efforts. And they may be right.

West Virginia, Pennsylvania, Michigan, Ohio, and New York are all trying some experiments to encourage people on welfare to participate in the labor market and to contribute more to society. More modest experimental efforts are taking place in almost two-thirds of the states.

Illinois has launched what it calls Project Chance, a program geared to training and job placement, similar to the programs in other states. Illinois is contracting for $3 million in job placement with the private sector, a not-so-subtle commentary on the lack of effectiveness they find in some of the public employment offices.

The City of Baltimore worked with federal officials in an area called Mt. Winans to rehabilitate public housing units, using people in the units to do it. Forty-one people were given six weeks of instruction. Twenty-six were women, fifteen men, and all started out at the minimum wage, slightly more than they were receiving on welfare. There was one supervisor for each four employees. Rules included: no drugs or alcohol on the job; if you showed up late for work, you had to go home; and you had to work until it was time to quit. After one year, one-fourth of those who started the program have failed. They were fired for inattendance or attitude problems. One is in jail. The manager of the project, Carnelious Harrison, says they ''feel they've contributed something to the community. They're proud of what they've done.'' He also noted that the children take great pride, pointing to the work and saying, ''Look what mama did.''[1]

State and community leaders throughout the nation understand the political unpopularity of spending money for welfare. Combine that with the proper yearning to do a better job of helping people, and you have the recipe for change that is stirring in the states. Some of what will happen—and is happening—is not good. Much of what will happen will be good.

These efforts will not be a substitute, however, for a Guaranteed Job Opportunity Program or a good education effort or other basics on which the states and nation must work. State leadership is important. More specifically, state experimentation is important. The nation can learn from these probes into new territory. But beyond the experimental role, research on what the states have done is far enough along that it is safe to say that even the finest job training and job search programs cannot have more than a modest impact. Because of limited resources and limited impact, the states can at best dance around the edges of the problem. It will take the federal government to march on the problem.

Endnotes

1. ''Hammers and Nails in Mt. Winans,'' by Kitty Krause, *Washington Monthly,* April 1986.

Chapter Seven

A Word for Communities with High Unemployment

UNEMPLOYMENT DOES NOT OCCUR in a nation or in a community accidentally, nor will it disappear by simply wishing it away. My experience working with many communities through the years should not surprise anyone: Those who work at it improve their situation, and those who sit around and sulk and hope for a General Motors plant to suddenly alight in their community are the losers.

A few recommendations, listed below, can help community leaders fight their unemployment problems.

Work at keeping the jobs you have now and getting existing businesses to expand.

To a great extent most communities are looking elsewhere for that four-leaf clover that is right at their feet. Remember that businesses are like people: They want to be wanted. Let them know their efforts are appreciated.

Hollywood Brands, a candy factory in Centralia, Illinois, burned down. Word spread that the parent corporation planned to rebuild in the South. The parent corporation, Consolidated Foods (now Sara Lee), was persuaded to hold off making the move to the South while some of us talked with them. Mayor Jack Sligar of Centralia got involved; the union leaders and other community leaders did also. They all played a key role. Finally, Consolidated Foods decided to rebuild Hollywood Brands in Centralia. It is now one of the most modern candy factories anywhere in the world, employing more than 300 people. If we had just accepted our fate when we heard that they were moving to another state, that would have ended those jobs for that community. A business was retained by being shown in concrete terms that they were wanted and needed. This is a significant story also in that John Bryan, the chief executive officer of Consolidated Foods, did not simply sit down at a table with a pencil and a computer and ask what looked good on paper for his company. That was part of it, but if that had been the whole picture, Centralia would have lost Hollywood Brands. Corporate officers also like to be good citizens. When he and others saw they were really wanted, they made a decision that has turned out to be the right one, both for their business and for the community involved. A community stretched itself to keep a business, and the business stretched itself to stay.

Also, remember: 80 percent of the new jobs created in this country over the next decade will be in small businesses. If a local business wants to increase its employment by two people, help that business. Most progress is not dramatic.

Be willing to stick your neck out.

No one is in the United States Senate today without taking risks. No one is even modestly successful in business without taking risks. A community that wants to move ahead but takes no risks is not likely to make significant headway.

LaSalle, Illinois, a community with high unemployment, had a few business leaders who put up a metal shell building to be developed and completed by any small industry they could bring in. One is now coming, employing ten people. A huge breakthrough? No. A significant breakthrough. Yes, but not simply because of the ten jobs, welcome as they are. More important, the LaSalle community learned that you can risk something and profit by it.

In 1985, the mental hospital at Manteno, Illinois, closed its doors. One of the largest such facilities in Illinois—seventy-five buildings on 350 acres—it was a source for 1,800 jobs for Manteno (population 2,864) and the surrounding area. State Senator Jeremiah Joyce put together a small group to discuss what could be done with the large facility. Some local people looked at it, began some creative thinking and acting. Led by local businessman Wayne Sims and the Smith brothers, they are starting to turn a heavy blow to their community into a great asset for their area and the state. It is not an accomplished deed yet, but already two industries have located on the land, a veterans home has been established, and significant announcements are in the offing. They will do it!

Herrin, Illinois, seemed the most unlikely community in southern Illinois to attract industry. It was not on a main state highway and did not have railroad service. But what it did have was some business leaders willing to stick their necks out. Clyde Brewster, a Chevrolet dealer, Jo Walker, who owned a men's clothing store, and others decided they were willing to sign notes at the local bank to create attractions for industries to locate in Herrin. For more than two decades—until the emergence of World Color Press plants in that area of the state—one of the most unlikely communities became the major industrial city of that region of Illinois. Thousands of jobs were created. The key: a few people willing to risk something. Another word for that is leadership.

Be creative.

Dixon, Illinois—the hometown of President Reagan—is moving ahead. Like most Illinois communities, it has had, and still has,

economic problems. One of their keys to turning things around
has been a small group of about a dozen people who get together
for a good mind-stretching, brainstorming session about what Dixon can do.

Here is an example of what has happened there. Dixon, population 15,701, has several families of Hmong refugees, people who
were mountain tribesmen in Laos and then escaped after the Vietnam conflict. The Hmong people have had more difficulty adjusting
than some southeast Asians and more of them have temporarily
ended up on welfare. Life in their mountains is very different from
life in the United States. But one of the merchants of Dixon was
having a hard time buying men's T-shirts. He discovered another
merchant in Dixon with the same problem. They got a sewing machine and material and hired one of the Hmong people to sew T-
shirts. When I was last in Dixon, they had more than twenty people employed making T-shirts at above the minimum wage rate.
They were in the process of borrowing money to get more sewing equipment. Being creative paid off.

One of the things a community brainstorming session should
look at is how you can convert community liabilities into assets.
That empty building—can it be converted into a small factory, or
be used by the local community college, or be used to attract a
company in another community that needs storage space? That
old schoolhouse, can it be converted into a restaurant that is unusual? Can the presence of an ethnic community with some problems be turned into more of a community asset? Can it be used
to attract foreign investment or to promote exports? The devastated
land nearby that is now useless because it was strip-mined for
coal—can it be converted into a community asset in some way?
A public housing project with crime problems can be a cause for
concern, or it can be the basis of a creative new approach to reduce
crime. Which do you want it to be?

Like many Illinois communities, Joliet's economy has dipped
substantially in recent years. Rev. James Riley and some other
people thought they would try something for the jobless. They

formed a foundation called Higher Horizons. They solicited old or unneeded equipment and unsaleable merchandise from businesses in the Joliet area, rehabilitating the equipment where possible, figuring imaginative ways of using the merchandise. "Someone's junk is someone's treasure," they say. And they accept not only equipment, they also accept businesses. The foundation's executive director describes their efforts: "Like Goodwill Industries, which takes unused, discarded clothing and helps someone stay warm, we'll channel corporate America's unwanted materials into the hands of people who need them.... In today's world of conglomerates, a corporation may find one subsidiary operating at below-cost efficiency. The business is marginal—not enough return for the money. Under the old system, the answer would be to sell the building, stock, and inventory, and lay off the people.... Under our program, we say, give the business to us and take your tax benefit by donating to a not-for-profit organization. What might not be a viable business to Amoco or AT&T would be a treasure for us. And we'll maintain those jobs."[1] They are also doing creative things to encourage small businesses to grow. They take everything from bricks to typewriters to lathes to printing presses to businesses. It's a new endeavor, and like many new endeavors, it is having its share of problems. But it is a creative approach to the community problem of unemployment. It is not *the* answer for there are no single answers, but it is one brick in building the structure of a better tomorrow for Joliet.

Look at the higher education possibilities.

Many of the communities that have moved ahead tied a university or community college or private college into their future. Get some of the practical people at the nearest higher education facility to meet with you informally to talk about growing together. It can be anything from a "business incubator"—a temporary home provided for a fledgling business, with technical help provided—that a community college operates to a more sophisticated tie-in like Princeton Research Park near Princeton University in New Jersey.

A handful of states have really moved effectively in combining the private sector and higher education. Most states, including my home state of Illinois, have not.

Improve your community.

Businesses and industries are not abstractions; they are people. And people like nice communities. They're interested not only in an adequate water and sewer system and fire protection. They are also interested in good schools, a fine library, stimulating cultural life, low crime rates, clean streets, well-maintained homes and business places—all the things that you associate with a fine community. I know of no exception to this rule: *A community that works at improving itself helps itself economically in the long run.* The payoff is usually not immediate, but it will come. If there is one thing that is crucial, it is a good school system. A community that wants industrial growth and has poor schools is not likely to experience growth.

After a struggle between many states involving local, state, and federal officials, the Chrysler-Mitsubishi plant decided to locate in the Bloomington-Normal, Illinois area, bringing more than 9,000 jobs to our state. After the arrangements had all been completed and signed, a top officer of Mitsubishi visited my office with some of his fellow officials from Japan. After the usual pleasantries, I asked what made him pick Bloomington-Normal. The state made a fine offer, he told me, and it is a beautiful community. I conceded that to him, but I said many states had made fine offers, and there are many beautiful communities. Yes, he told me, but Bloomington had something else. More than twenty-five years ago, Bloomington began a sister-city relationship with a city in Japan. About three years ago, a school in Bloomington—a community with two universities—started teaching Japanese. "We felt we would be welcomed there," he told me.

People in Bloomington-Normal who set up a sister-city relationship and decided to enrich their culture by teaching their children

Japanese not only helped themselves culturally, they helped themselves economically.

Believe in yourself.

Some years ago leaders in a community in Illinois asked me to help them develop the economy of their county. We set up a meeting of the local Rotary Club, Woman's Club, and other civic groups. I asked three outside business leaders to visit the county and then join me that night at a dinner. I asked each business leader to toss out ideas to the group as to what might be done. After each idea someone in the audience would respond, "That won't work here because. . ." If you believe it won't work, it won't. Every community has its share of village nags, people who always see the negative side of everything, who are sure that things won't work. If that type of element becomes too strong in a community, it is paralyzing. Believe in yourself.

Endnotes

1. Letter of Rev. James Riley to Paul Simon, Mar. 6, 1986.

Chapter Eight

The Last, Brief Word

If the question is "Can America provide jobs for everyone able and willing to work," the answer is unambiguously yes.

If the question is "Has America provided jobs for everyone able and willing to work?," the answer is just as unambiguously no.

—Economist Lester Thurow[1]

THERE WAS A TIME when people considered to be knowledgeable simply understood that an eight-hour day was unachievable. They knew that prohibiting ten-year-olds from working in factories was "pie in the sky." These same types of experts knew that whooping cough and polio were the inevitable lot of humanity. And, of course, they knew that passing a law to permit blacks to vote everywhere in this nation and to go into restaurants and hotels would never be tolerated and would never come about.

But a few people with dreams and vision and practicality changed these assumptions.

Now it is "common knowledge" that guaranteeing all Americans a job opportunity is unachievable. They are as wrong as their predecessors were.

I am not interested in changing the myth; I am interested in changing the reality. We can create a nation in which every American has the opportunity to take pride in his or her contribution. Political leadership will either move us in that direction or continue the aimless drifting that is gradually denying the American dream to more and more of our citizens. People denied the opportunity to work face the choice of welfare or theft to survive. They deserve a better choice. Instead of taking the next great step forward for this nation, the guarantee of a job opportunity, we are engaged in a mammoth public non-works program.

Political leadership can be short-sighted, basically defending the status quo, appealing to the selfish "me first" instinct in each of us, telling us indirectly to "hold onto what you have." Or, leadership can take the longer view. It can provide a vision of a better tomorrow rather than clinging tenaciously to a yesterday that cannot be repeated. It can appeal to the noble in us, rather than the greed in us. It can help us build a better America for all our citizens.

But political leadership is often—change that to *usually*—cautious. There must be at least a small base of people who share a dream and a hope. I want you to be one of those. It is not enough to have a small group of people in Washington, D.C., aware that our policy desperately needs improvement and can be turned around. That change will require interest and support in Kalamazoo and Newark and Lake Bluff and Ventura and all over grass roots America. The general recognition of the seriousness of the problem, and that it can be solved, is not out there yet. The lack of public concern is reflected in a lack of serious concern by most policy-makers. You can help change that by doing five things.

First, write to the Paul Douglas Foundation, 1140 19th Street, N.W., Suite 601, Washington, D.C., 20036, and to the National Committee for Full Employment, 815 16th Street, N.W., Washington, D.C., 20006. Tell both of them you would like some information and material and that you want to help. Ask for information about the idea of a guaranteed job program.

Second, write to your member of the House and to your two senators, and tell them that you would like to guaranteee a job opportunity to every American. Tell them that is essential to having a nation that is more productive and more competitive with the rest of the world.

Third, send a letter to the editor of your local newspaper or newspapers urging that our policy be changed so that we develop our human potential more. In most newspapers, letters to the editor are read more than the editorials—and are read more by political leaders, also. Be specific in your letter about what you would like to see happen.

Fourth, get your church or synagogue group, your Kiwanis Club or Junior League Club, your labor union or citizen action group to use one of their programs to discuss some aspect of this problem and what citizens can do about it.

Fifth, pick one item in this book on which you would like to work. Flip through the pages quickly to decide what it is and then talk it over with two of your friends. Then act.

You and I are blessed with living in a great and good country. But it can become a much better country.

With your help.

Endnotes

1. Lester Thurow, *The Zero-Sum Solution* (New York: Simon and Schuster, 1985), p. 314.

POSTSCRIPT

Advice to the Unemployed
(and the Employed)

UNEMPLOYMENT IS SOMETHING that happens to someone else. But people unexpectedly find themselves in this category. What should you do if you find yourself out of a job? The same steps that are good for the unemployed are good for the employed. While the need is not pressing for those working, things can be done that make future unemployment less likely; and if it occurs, it is not likely to be as lengthy a time of unemployment as it otherwise would be. Circumstances differ, but these six steps are sound for those out of work (and for others).

Ask yourself what you would really like to do.

People do a good job at something they enjoy. What would you really like to be doing in a year or in five years? Then take prac-

tical steps to move in that direction. We all have to do some things
we don't like, but life is too short to spend all our lives doing something we do not enjoy.

Volunteer.

If your church or synagogue needs someone to help with a spring
clean-up, be a volunteer. If the local Boosters Club or Methodist
Church asks for help for a community project, be that volunteer.
If your PTA needs people to assist with a chicken dinner, volunteer.
If the National Association for the Advancement of Colored People or the League of United Latin American Citizens needs people
to solicit memberships, be one of those people. What volunteer-
ing gives you is two things: A sense of doing something useful
and meaningful—important for all of us but particularly for the
unemployed—and it puts you into contact with other people. Why
is the latter important? Many jobs—almost a majority—are filled
through word passing from one person to another about a job opening or a person seeking a position. Tell others simply, "If you
hear of something, let me know. I'd sure appreciate it." The word
will spread that you are looking for a job, and that's good. Being
a volunteer also looks good on a resume. For those already employed, the more people you meet and know, the greater the likelihood that you can be of help to others or that they can be of help
to you. A quick glance at the list of people who work in my office
suggests that about one-fifth were people who *volunteered* to
help—free of charge—in one capacity or another. They made a
good enough impression that as we put our staff together, their
combination of interests and skills made them the preferred employees. Casual contacts that you make can create a great difference
in your life. The president of one of this nation's largest corporations moved into that opportunity because of a contact he made
at a Christian Science Sunday School class. In this life you never
have too many friends; you can have too few. Volunteer! Do the
things that bring you into contact with others. Educational research
has come to this not surprising conclusion: High school students

who combine academic studies with extracurricular activities are more successful in college. We could change that slightly: People who engage in activities outside their work—or lack of it— gain experience that contributes to their success in life.

Improve yourself.

If you have not received your high school diploma, study for a high school equivalency test and get it. If you do not speak a foreign language, learn one. If you have an evening free each week and the local community college offers a course that interests you, take it. If you know nothing about classical music, start enriching yourself. Employers are impressed by people who have varied interests and knowledge, not by those who are one-dimensional.

If you can, plant a garden.

This may seem to be a small thing, and because of the season or because of where you live, you may not be able to do this. But if you can, do it. It will save you a few dollars, provide fresh food but, most important, you will have the feeling and the knowledge that you are contributing something. To avoid the sense of being useless is extremely important. If your circumstances don't permit you to plant a garden, find another constructive alternative.

Get help from others.

Ask others for suggestions on how you might get a job. Even talking to other people out of work can be helpful, learning what those people do to try to get jobs. Also, talk to people who are more successful, getting their suggestions and ideas. This can give you valuable insights. It could be a friend who is now working. It could be your minister, priest or rabbi. Talking to others about your job pursuit not only can be helpful in getting a job, it can improve your outlook. Unloading our problems on someone else is something we all need occasionally.

   Getting help from others is true not only for getting a job, but for the host of practical problems you will face being unemployed:

paying the gas bill, making the rent or mortgage payments, getting clothes for your children. The line between sharing your needs with others and begging is sometimes thin, but it is important for you and for others that they undersand the problems you face.

Don't give up.

Part of the problem with being out of work is that you start to get down on yourself and down on everything. And when you get down on everyone else, they start to get down on you. Sometimes keeping up your spirits is not easy. In our society we tend to blame the person who is out of work, and sometimes it is a personal failing, but more frequently it is the simple reality that there are too few jobs to go around. That is your fault only to the extent that you have joined almost all Americans in tolerating a public policy that permits this. But blaming yourself for your lack of a job won't help you or anyone else. I had a friend who had cancer, and I called the hospital to ask how he was doing. The hospital responded that he was not in his room because he was out cheering up all the other cancer patients! That's the spirit that is needed. That's easy for me to write, difficult for you to do, I know. But please try.

These simple suggestions may help. I have seen them work.

I do not suggest that getting a job is easy. If you are unemployed, you know better than that.

I do suggest that you work hard at it, and I also ask you to work at helping to change national policy so that you and others do not have to go through the pain of unemployment without greater protection than is now available.

If you can help to change national policy, you will have served people for generations to come.

Index